ANCIENT MEXICO IN COLOUR

Pyramid of Quetzalcoatl, Teotihuacán (*Caption on page 158*)

ANCIENT MEXICO IN COLOUR

Text by

IGNACIO BERNAL

Photographs by

IRMGARD GROTH

60 plates in Colour

McGRAW-HILL BOOK COMPANY · NEW YORK

PHOTOLITHOS SUPPLIED BY CLICHÉS SCHWITTER AG ZURICH

PRINTED IN SWITZERLAND BY IMPRIMERIE PAUL ATTINGER SA NEUCHÂTEL

BOUND IN GERMANY BY KARL HANKE · DUSSELDORF

LIBRARY OF CONGRESS CATALOG CARD NUMBER: 68-19684

04905

THE PLATES

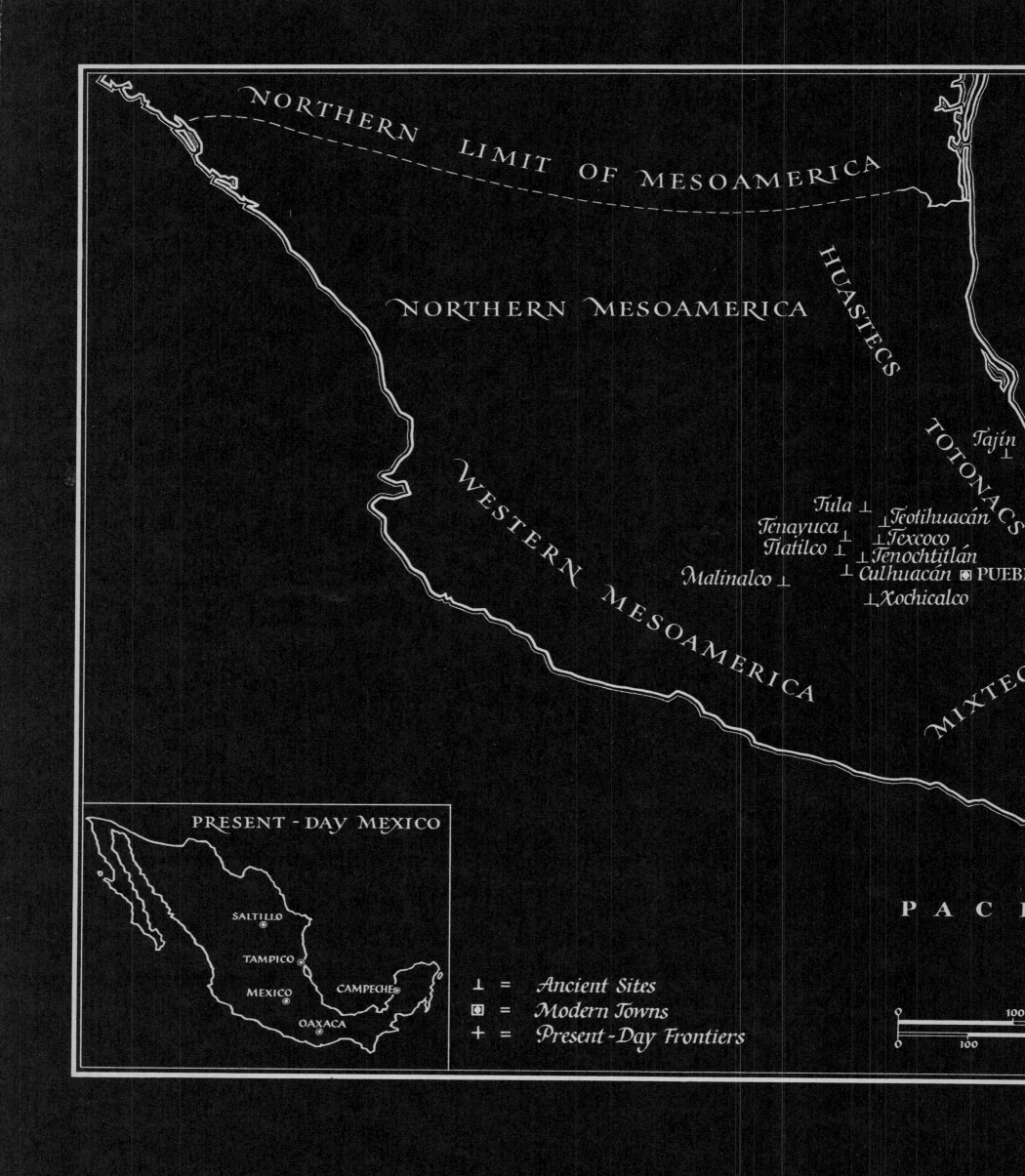

NORTHERN LIMIT OF MESOAMERICA

NORTHERN MESOAMERICA

HUASTECS

TOTONACS

Tajín ⊥

WESTERN MESOAMERICA

Tula ⊥ ⊥ Teotihuacán
Tenayuca ⊥ ⊥ Texcoco
Tlatilco ⊥ ⊥ Tenochtitlán
Malinalco ⊥ ⊥ Culhuacán ⊡ PUEB
⊥ Xochicalco

MIXTEC

PRESENT - DAY MEXICO

SALTILLO ⊙

TAMPICO ⊙

MEXICO ⊙   CAMPECHE ⊙

OAXACA ⊙

PACI

⊥ = Ancient Sites
⊡ = Modern Towns
+ = Present-Day Frontiers

100

100

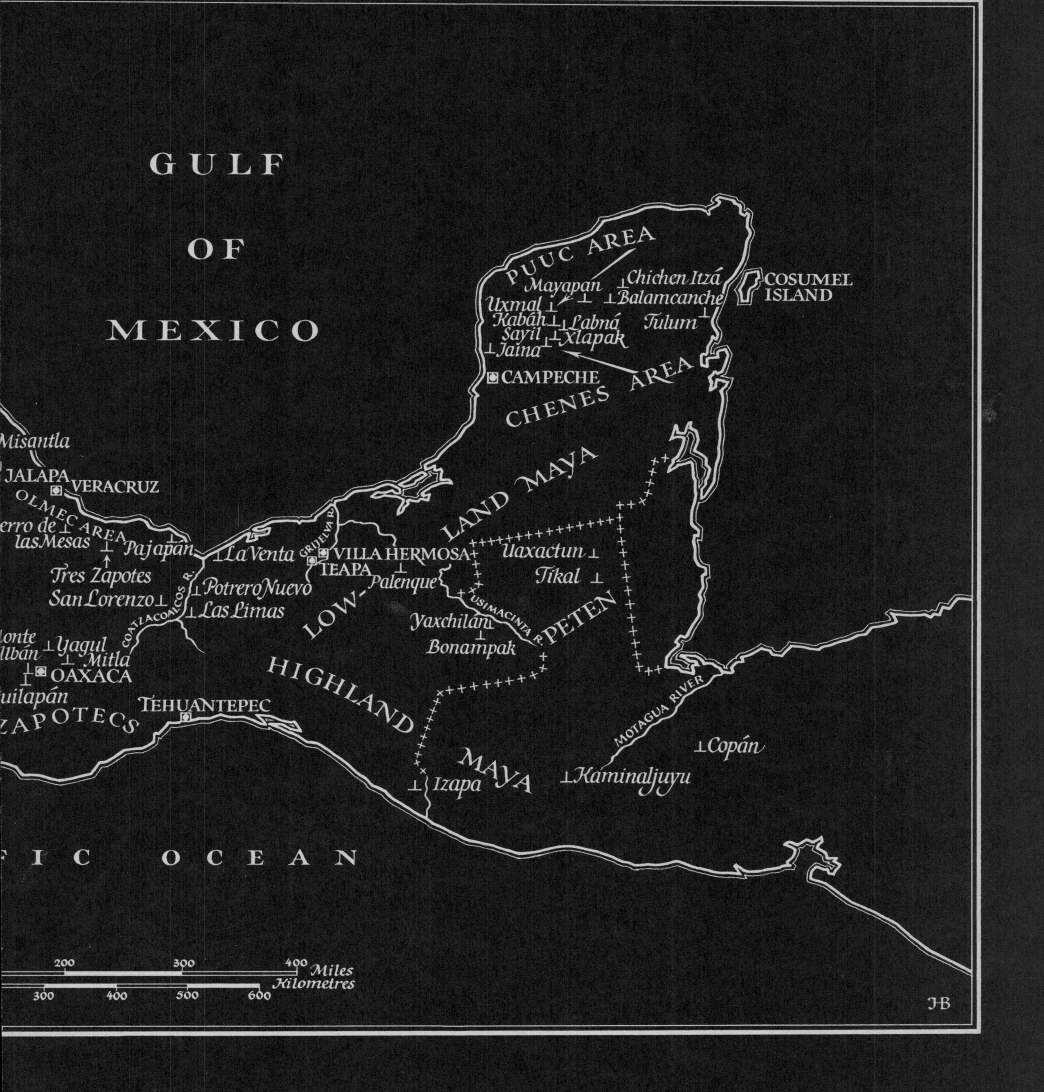

GULF

OF

MEXICO

Misantla

◉ JALAPA ◉ VERACRUZ

OLMEC AREA

erro de
las Mesas ⊥ *Pajapán*

Tres Zapotes
San Lorenzo ⊥

Potrero Nuevo
⊥ *Las Limas*

lonte ⊥ *Yagul*
lbán ⊥ *Mitla*
⊥ ◉ OAXACA

uilapán

ZAPOTECS TEHUANTEPEC

HIGHLAND

PUUC AREA

Mayapan ⊥ *Chichen Itzá* COSUMEL
ISLAND
Uxmal ⊥ ⊥ *Balamcanche*
Kabáh ⊥ ⊥ *Labná* *Tulum* ⊥
Sayil ⊥ ⊥ *Xlapak*
⊥ *Jaina*
◉ CAMPECHE CHENES AREA

LAND MAYA

⊥ La Venta GRIJELVA R.
⊥ ◉ VILLA HERMOSA *Uaxactun* ⊥
TEAPA
⊥ *Palenque* *Tikal* ⊥

Yaxchilán ⊥ PETEN
Bonampak

LOW-

MAYA

⊥ *Izapa*

Kaminaljuyu

MOTAGUA RIVER

⊥ *Copán*

'FIC OCEAN

200   300   400 *Miles*
                                  Kilometres
300   400   500   600

J·B

The Olmecs and the Beginnings
of Urban Life

IN A FAMOUS SENTENCE 'URBEM ROMAM A PRINCIPIO REGES HABUERI' Tacitus dismissed centuries of Roman antiquity. I believe he felt that these early periods had little to do with the story that was to follow, the story he really wanted to tell. For the same reason, a few—if less famous—paragraphs will suffice to cover the many millennia before the advent of civilisation in Ancient Mexico. Historically, however, we should think, not in terms of ancient Mexico, but of Mesoamerica—that part of the American continent comprising the southern half of Mexico and all the Central American countries as far as Western Honduras and Nicaragua. This is the area that was to see, towards the beginning of the first millennium B.C., the rise of a civilisation whose history will be outlined in the pages that follow. As the name of this book suggests, however, I concern myself principally with the Mexican part of Mesoamerica, omitting the marginal provinces to the west and north.

Long before my story begins, man had settled the continent, migrating from Asia in a succession of waves. This resulted in a considerable diversity of physical types among the later inhabitants. Though they all belong to the same race we find both broad and narrow heads, small and prominent noses, tall and squat bodies, and an infinite number of gradations over the large expanse of the Americas. A variety of tribal languages were spoken.

Cultural advance in this period before the formation of urban communities, though slow, was marked; it resulted, in the course of time, in improved farming methods, saw the development of scraggy wild plants into cultivated species: corn, the most important of all, beans, squash, many fruits and vegetables, minor seed crops and cotton. A few animals such as the dog and the turkey were domesticated—the latter one of the great gifts of the American

Indian to *haute cuisine*. The stability produced by regular crops not only allowed a certain security, and time for other pursuits, but obliged man to remain in the same locality all the year round, or nearly so. After untold adventures man had become a farmer; he now built modest houses of mud and wood and grass; he discovered the arts of pottery, weaving and stone polishing. Slowly villages grew. The tribal pattern emerged and with it the shaman, forerunner of the priest, since his magic was the prototype of later religion. The world of ideas and beliefs was being fashioned along lines that were to become the core of Mesoamerican civilisation.

And so the stage is set and men are ready to ring up the curtain on the first act of civilised life. The setting is a small corner of Mesoamerica: the flat, humid, tropical alluvial plain of southern Veracruz and northern Tabasco. Short but swift-flowing rivers cross and frequently flood a large part of the land. Elsewhere in Mesoamerica water was always at a premium and the gods had to be constantly invoked for this gift of the heavens, here there was too much of it. Of course there was hardly any stone and the dense jungle, if left to itself, easily suffocated any human effort at cultivation. Nevertheless, the anonymous people living here—whom we call the Olmecs because in later times the area bore that name, which signifies land of rubber—managed to take the first great step towards civilised living.

Of the many places that have been excavated in this region, three have proved to be particularly important: La Venta, Tres Zapotes and San Lorenzo. They are all largish sites showing various stages of urban planning, rather vague at the last-mentioned two but quite distinct at La Venta, where it is not only precise but clearly antecedent to future Mesoamerican cities. Mounds—once topped by temples—were built around plazas in a regular pattern. Furthermore, the whole ceremonial area was ranged along a central axis running very nearly north–south. This imaginary line of La Venta was to become a real line—a street—in the case of Teotihuacán in the highlands. Thus, not only had the planned city been devised by about 800 B.C., but it had been given the general north–south orientation that was to become customary later on. This laying-out of cities in relation to the cardinal points is highly characteristic of ancient Indian thought and exemplifies one of the basic traits of their civilisation: ceremonialism, a positive mania for order and ritual which pervades it from the start. This feature alone would be indication enough that with the Olmecs we already have the emerging pattern of Meso-america and not simply a tribal society.

9

The buildings themselves are quite unimpressive. Made of earth or adobe, they hardly ever contain stone—which, as mentioned, is practically non-existent in the area and therefore a great luxury—or mortar or stucco, materials which were still unknown. Yet the main pyramid at La Venta—the tallest of the period known to us—is nearly 100 feet high even without the temple, which has entirely disappeared. A number of smaller buildings surround the pyramid and near by was a tomb made of huge natural pillars of basalt that had been brought from a great distance. This tomb—the only one of its type ever found and the only stone construction at the site—suggests an elaboration on what must have been the ordinary house or temple. These will have been made of wooden poles; but none has come down to us, having rotted away long since. Basalt pillar construction is much too costly and too limited in its application to have been successful, and as far as we know was never repeated in later cultures and used only sparingly among the Olmecs.

If their architecture is quite primitive and scarcely allows us to consider the Olmec world as civilised, or nearly so, their striking monumental stone sculpture—unbelievable for the time and place—is astonishing. It shows an already elaborate organisation which enabled them to quarry and transport over great distances those enormous blocks of stone that were fashioned into colossal heads, altars, stelae, chests and sarcophagi, human or animal representations, all of such quality that were it not for indisputable evidence regarding their age we might place them not at the beginning of ancient American art but at its end.

These monoliths, frequently of vast proportions, were undoubtedly carved locally even if the stones had been brought from far away. We have no means of telling how many have been lost forever or how many more are still buried in the jungle and marshes of southern Veracruz. *Plate 2* Hardly a year passes without a new discovery. Twelve colossal heads are now known, from three *Plate 4* sites, and nine huge rectangular monoliths that we call altars. Carved on the surfaces of the latter, some in high relief, are men, some of whom are holding children in their arms in a sort of cere-monial rite as though the elders were presenting to the people the small, important 'heir to the throne' or a victim for sacrifice. A smaller altar from Potrero Nuevo shows two human figures supporting a table. It is to my knowledge the earliest example of atlantes, a type of figure that was to be repeated continuously in later cultures.

Stelae of various shapes and types occur fairly frequently. Some—enormous and finely carved—show one, two or more central figures, occasionally surrounded with little dwarfs which are perhaps the legendary *chaneques* or evil spirits. A particularly beautiful example from La Venta depicts a man sitting among the coils of a huge vicious-looking serpent, perhaps a first version of what was to become a principal theme: Quetzalcoatl, the feathered serpent. Stelae and their associated altars were to become a regular feature of Maya art; they are also relatively frequent in Oaxaca and Veracruz, but rarely found in the highland cities. Yet, even if the Maya inherited this Olmec trait and elaborated it to a remarkable extent, it is quite apparent that their stelae are more pictorial—as though derived from painting—than the Olmec stelae which are clearly the work of sculptors and the product of a culture that had not attained to a knowledge of mural frescoes.

The Olmecs carved a large number of statues in the round resembling human beings, or of men with animal features, mainly jaguar. In nearly every case naked men—without primary *Plate 3* sexual attributes—are depicted. They sometimes wear a loin-cloth or a belt. The asexuality and the fact that men only are portrayed are typical Olmec traits; their contemporaries, who did not carve stone to any comparable degree, made feminine figurines of clay.

All these human figures together with the smaller figurines in jade or stone, besides representing a major aesthetic achievement, give us a general idea of what the Olmecs looked like. Owing to the extreme acidity of the soil not a single skeleton has been recovered in sufficiently good shape to permit anthropological analysis. Thus we are able to judge their appearance only from their art.

In many ways the smaller figures, mostly carved in those wonderful varieties of jadeite so dear to the Olmec sculptor, convey still better their ideal of human beauty. Besides the traits already mentioned they show artificially produced 'embellishments', such as the deformation of the skull and filing of the teeth. The extraordinary avocado-shaped heads, frequent in figurines, were achieved by binding the new-born infant in special ways and must have been regarded as highly desirable.

Other deformations shown in art are entirely fanciful and are far removed from living individuals or aesthetic ideals but fulfil religious needs. For instance the frequent groove in the centre of the skull, by nature impossible in the human head, is perhaps taken from a similar feature apparent in the jaguar. Others are clearly a result of the combination of jaguar and human

11

traits; these are carried so far that we sometimes can hardly tell whether a human or a beast is intended. This intimate association of man and jaguar is one of the most typical Olmec cultural traits and certainly a basic religious motif. We shall have more to say about this later on.

In many instances other deformed figures are shown: dwarfs, hunchbacks, men suffering from glandular defects, obesity and deafness. Interest in sickness or abnormality appears as another Olmec trait that was to last all through Mesoamerican history and which we find in most local cultures at different times.

Nevertheless, even with these deviations from human standards, the Olmecs are perhaps the only Mesoamerican people to have been interested in the beauty of the human body. Occasional statues show the play of muscle under the skin and there is a clear, if still rather primitive, delight in anatomical detail.

Although Olmec dress is extremely scanty, adornment is quite elaborate and includes most of the types that were to be worn for centuries to come. Great headdresses, ear-plugs, necklaces and bracelets are all represented. They were made of jade, stone, clay, and probably of wood and other perishable materials.

Nothing remains of the houses of the Olmecs, their way of life, their textiles or basketwork, the skins of the animals they used, or even their implements of bone or shell. It is quite certain that a large number of everyday objects or even ceremonial ones were made of wood, since this was the most readily available material. The stone for the great monuments or the jade for the small figures could have been obtained only with the greatest difficulty and effort, and it is indeed remarkable that it was in the very material which was lacking in their area that they accomplished their outstanding work—work on which their main claim to fame rests. Had they not imported these stones and carved such wonderful statues, we would consider the Olmecs as just another group among the many that peopled what was to become Mesoamerica, and not the initiators of civilisation in this part of the world.

Obviously neither Olmec economy nor Olmec art could have flourished in that repeatedly flooded land if some means of importing food and stone had not been found. This object they seem to have achieved through commerce or tribute. The Olmecs were, of course, well placed to bring things from outside by canoes or rafts drifting down stream, although transportation will have been far more difficult in the reverse direction. And we must remember that commerce is a two-way process. If you import objects you have to give something in exchange. What did the Olmecs give? Probably religious beliefs and certainly manufactured goods; this is one of the reasons for the widespread occurrence over nearly all of Mesoamerica of the small, sometimes beautifully made Olmec works of art that were traded in ancient times, either to obtain food or the materials that they needed.

But if Olmecs in fact initiated a tradition that was carried on by all later pre-Columbian cultures in Mesoamerica, then Olmec commercial dealings must be reflected by those of the Aztecs—the only peoples about which we have considerable information through writings of the early Colonial period, to supplement the archaeological findings. Such dealings were based not on peace or friendly barter but on conquest: in other words, on war. Numerous indications, none sufficiently strong by themselves but rather conclusive if considered together, show that the Olmecs certainly had recourse to arms, and actually seem to have been the inventors of the war–conquest–tribute pattern that was to prevail all through Mesoamerican history.

They probably gained two sorts of outside footholds. Some seem to have been real colonies: a group of Olmec soldiers, and perhaps even Olmec families would establish themselves in one or more localities of an area by subjecting the primitive and weaker inhabitants, by virtue of their superior strength and knowledge. These local cultures would then practically disappear, with the result that only Olmec-inspired objects remain for us to find. This is exemplified by Tlatilco in the Central Valley of Mexico. In other cases the Olmecs were not real conquerors. They simply imposed their will through expanding religious control or military ascendency over other provinces, but without their permanent physical presence. This seems to have been their method when they were not dealing with simple folk, as in the Valley of Mexico, but with quite evolved cultures, in many ways more advanced than the Olmecs themselves, as in the case of Monte Albán or of Guatemala. We cannot distinguish today between objects which were the result of commercial transactions and those which represent tribute from a conquered people, or even perhaps from people who were not conquered but in some way feared the Olmec soldier or the Olmec priest.

Of course we know nothing of their armies or their possible military triumphs, but if there was such a thing as an Olmec state it is most unlikely that it could have been kept going, still less have continued to expand, without military action. We have some vague intimations of this in such places as, for instance, Altar IV at La Venta, or Monument C at Tres Zapotes, which relate scenes of war and conquest.

We are also unable to guess what the Olmec state was like, what authority it exercised, and whether it was ruled by one person, or several. Most probably, since this is the typical Mesoamerican pattern, a group of priests and high military chieftains formed the élite, the small aristocratic group who governed the majority. We must remember also that the usual distinction between priest and head of state or military war lord does not apply in Mesoamerica; although of course there were professional priests and professional soldiers, very frequently one man was equipped to function as both.

The priest derived his prestige from the fact that he was in a way the intermediary between the people and the gods or the heavenly powers. He was also the man in whom culture was vested and, as happened in later times, the one who knew how to read and write, who knew the calendar, could predict the eclipses and the movements of the planets, who could determine the time for sowing or reaping, and who could even foretell the fate of each individual.

The ability to write huge numbers, in other words to use a system that allowed numbering by position, was only acquired very late in Olmec culture, actually at the very end of it. It is unlikely that the Olmecs were the sole inventors of the system; in all probability it slowly evolved from the combined thinking of the Metropolitan Olmecs and the inhabitants of certain places like Monte Albán or of centres in Chiapas and Guatemala which were part of the Olmec world but at the same time had their own high culture.

Writing, on any appreciable scale, appears for the first time on stone in Monte Albán. Did the people of the Valley of Oaxaca invent this most important instrument of civilisation? It is hard to tell, but they were certainly, as far as we know, the first to use it. These ancestors of the Zapotecs seem to have been not only the inventors of writing and of the calendar, but the first people to build monuments of stone; so in a way they were also the originators of architecture.

The first period of Monte Albán coincides with the great period of Olmec culture. The two are related in a number of ways, although they were separate entities and neither actually copied the other. However, influence flows mainly from the Olmec area into the Valley of Oaxaca. Of course, by Monte Albán culture we really mean the whole area of the Central Valley of Oaxaca. An incomplete survey of the region shows that in these three great valleys which converge in one place, only a single culture prevailed at any given moment. They constitute one of the clearest examples of an ecological area that is also a cultural area. As soon as the frontiers are passed, the culture changes; but within them—that is, surrounded by the high mountains—the people seem to have been quite homogeneous. If the sites differ, it is mainly a matter of degree; we cannot expect the large ones with an urban culture to resemble the small rural hamlets.

We know of very few monuments of the Monte Albán I period but enough to tell us that stone architecture was quite developed and the techniques of building well understood. Vertical walls and large staircases without balustrades were prevalent. Some walls were faced with large slabs of stone on which a human figure was carved in relief, generally in a distorted position—hence the name *Danzante,* 'Dancing Figures'. They are all male, just as in the Olmec *Plate 5* world. As with the Olmecs, too, they are nearly always shown nude. Nevertheless, except in rare instances, the sex is not apparent, although it is frequently transformed into a hieroglyph showing perhaps mutilation or some sort of sacrifice. Around many of these figures, or even on them, are glyphs, but these we cannot as yet decipher. They most probably refer to the name of the individual, or even in some cases perhaps to a village or an area that had been conquered by the people of Monte Albán I. Almost more eloquent still are those slabs that bear, not human figures but long rows of hieroglyphs, frequently accompanied by numerals. It is the beginning of a system of recording dates and perhaps commemorating historical occurrences, an idea that was to develop considerably and lead later to the Mayan stelae.

Not only in Monte Albán but in most of the Oaxacan area we find relics of that most characteristic religious feature of the Olmec world, the cult of the jaguar. We have already spoken of human figures associated with this animal. It seems to have been the only god—if that is a concept we can apply at this early date—or at least the most important single element in Olmec religion, and in Olmec religious expansion. This again points to the typical association or frequent combination of the soldier and the priest, and even the merchant. We do not know the Indian name for Monte Albán, but it is possible that it meant the Hill of the Jaguar.

Why did this animal become so important, and why in Olmec art is it so frequently depicted with human traits or as a human being with jaguar traits? A few statues, unfortunately very shattered and difficult to interpret correctly, seem to suggest copulation between a woman and a jaguar. Perhaps it was believed that these two begot the Olmec people, that they were therefore half human and half jaguar, that the jaguar was the totem of the group, and in many instances the essential element of their religion. All the other animals which were to become so important later had little significance at this time. Neither are the combinations of these and the large pantheon which was to spring up in all areas after the eclipse of the Olmec world yet in evidence. From the very little information we possess it is safe to say that the gods were not 'born' in southern Veracruz. On the other hand a number of clay urns in the Monte Albán I culture already represent certain ancient deities, although as yet with little of the regalia that was to distinguish them in later times.

The jaguar of the Olmecs seems to have been intimately connected with children, or with childish beings such as the *chaneques* in which people still believe today. These are old dwarfs with baby faces, who molest women and pester people, live in waterfalls, cause sickness, sometimes even feed on human brains. They bring the rains and often have magical powers over land animals and fishes. Not always as menacing as they would seem, all they frequently do is to play jokes, and rather bad ones at that. They can easily be got rid of by throwing water over them. Their association with rain is particularly important since they seem to be an early and still rather rudimentary form of Tlaloc, the great rain god so important and so necessary in dry areas that we see him represented more than any other divinity in later cultures. At Tenochtitlán his temple found a place next to that of the god of war in the great pyramid. Of course by that time he is associated more with the serpent than with the jaguar. This transformation seems to have taken place at the beginning of the Classic period practically everywhere in Mesoamerica. Perhaps this is due to the fact that the serpent is more ubiquitous an animal, whereas the jaguar only inhabits the hot lowlands.

Mesoamerican religion is intimately linked with sacrifice. In different ways this is probably true of every religion. All the same, in the Olmec world we have no direct proof of the existence of such a ritual. There are some indications that it may have already been in use but if so, it was probably on a minor scale and may not have been human sacrifice at all, except, as was to happen in later times, of children and dwarfs whose tears would placate the god of rain through a magic affinity.

We can recognise three major periods in this dawn of civilisation. The first, from 1200 to 800 B.C., is the preparatory period, directly antecedent but with the ingredients not yet set. Between 800 and 400 B.C. Olmec culture attains to the level of civilisation. This is the golden age when all the great sculpture and all the major advances, except writing, were made, not *Plates 6, 7* only in the Metropolitan Olmec area but also in other places, such as the Valley of Oaxaca, the Highlands of Guatemala, and probably the Pacific Coast.

By 400 B.C. the Metropolitan area seems to be on the downward path. Slowly buildings are abandoned and no more stone monuments are erected except on rare occasions. Yet between this date and 100 B.C. the first inscription in the Long Count appears, on Stela C at Tres Zapotes. It and other confusing but obviously very ancient inscriptions found both in Chiapas and in Guatemala prove that not only writing—already long established in Monte Albán, as we have seen—but also long calendrical inscriptions and especially numeration by position were already well understood. These major advances, oddly enough, are associated with the end of Olmec history.

From this time on, the Olmec area loses all importance. It was never again to be in the forefront of civilisation, though a large number of other local cultures were to draw inspiration from their notable antecedent.

To what causes is it possible to ascribe Olmec decline? Many theories have been propounded but none seems to provide a definite answer. If we accept that Olmec history followed the same pattern that later great cultures in Mesoamerica were to exhibit, with the usual cycle of birth, development, maturity and decadence, then we might conclude that the cause of Olmec deterioration was not basically economic. It would seem to have resulted, not from failing crops, climatic changes or the like, but from social pressures. The group of priests and leaders who had brought the Olmec people from modest beginnings to wealth and prosperity probably changed, as usually happens, from a creative minority into a dominant one. Several things suggest this, as for example the great tomb at La Venta, obviously built for a priest who had become a dictator in the manner of the pharaohs. In time the people instead of deriving benefits, ideas and guidance from this ruling élite—which would have made them willing to obey it—became bound in servitude to it. Rebellion in one form or another may have been the cause of the gradual dissolution of the ruling group, which in turn ultimately led to the collapse of Olmec high culture, once it had been taken out of their hands and fallen into those of the ignorant

17

masses. The cultural legacy bequeathed by the Olmecs would seem to have split into two main channels: one ran from the Isthmus of Tehuantepec southwards into what was broadly speaking the Maya world, the other from the Isthmus northwards, representing mainly the culture that developed in the Central Valleys, in Oaxaca and in Veracruz.

The Olmec inheritance was not necessarily transmitted by direct and obvious means. For instance, some features like the stela with an altar in front passed from the Olmecs through Izapa and the Lowland area bordering the Pacific into the Maya world; other features, perhaps the cult of the jaguar itself, seem also to stem from here. Then again there were many that either died out with the Olmecs or took a different form because they became mixed with local roots that had during this time also been evolving. Thus the Maya world or the world of Teotihuacán cannot be explained in terms of their Olmec ancestry, no matter how much this may have contributed. The local development is important, so important that it is the basic one, and the Olmecs are only a sort of ferment that led them on to this more developed stage. The essential contribution of the Olmecs lay in establishing the cultural mould to which other cultures in Mesoamerica would adapt themselves all through the rest of its history. They laid out the roads along which future merchants would pass. Their warriors pioneered the areas that later soldiers would occupy, and prepared the way for other élites who would devise new methods and systems; they also established the religious pattern. Above all, a specific area from the Panuco River to Nicaragua was now separated from the rest of the American continent and reached a higher step on the road to civilisation. Mesoamerica had come into being.

OLMEC HEAD FROM LA VENTA.   Plate 2

OLMEC HEAD
FROM LA VENTA
Plate 2

These massive heads, some measuring up to 3 metres in height, are one of the triumphs of Olmec art. Up to now they have been found only in the three principal Olmec cities—La Venta, Tres Zapotes, and San Lorenzo. They are not fragments since they never had bodies—a concept which was to be used again 2,000 years later in Aztec sculpture.

The Olmec heads are among the most characteristic representations of this style, not only because of their enormous size, but also because they reflect what these people regarded as the ideal of beauty. Heavy faces with wide noses and thick lips are realistic portrayals, being directly inspired by the faces of the people themselves, and some have taken the heads to be portraits of chiefs or important personages. The resemblance between the various heads in any one city is so great that it might be thought that they depict the same face. This would suggest a god, were it not that individual deities had not yet appeared in the Olmec world. That they represent ritually decapitated ball players seems equally unlikely. Their function and purpose remain a mystery, and today they stand in the jungle, bearing witness only to the extraordinary skill of their anonymous sculptors.

The monoliths of the Olmec area are found on an alluvial plain where stone does not exist. Therefore the stone used for carving the twelve known heads, the altars, and other pieces of sculpture had to be brought from a considerable distance, which is astonishing for that period. Maybe rafts or canoes were used to carry it down the rivers which flow towards the region. Such a feat indicates a highly developed social organisation, and probably a central power with sufficient authority to command such lavish expenditure of labour.

SCULPTURE
FROM MISANTLA
Plate 3

The human figure is one of the basic themes used in Olmec sculpture. More than twenty figures are known, very diverse as to quality, size and period. In every case it is men who are represented; it appears that women were not regarded as suitable subjects. Clothed or nude—the latter is more common—they betray an unmistakable style; so much so, that even when the head is missing, as in this large piece from Misantla—now in the Museum of Jalapa—the body alone enables us to recognise the culture to which it belongs. The most frequent posture shows a man seated with legs crossed in oriental fashion with the arms resting on them, as in this instance. The figure almost always wears a loin-cloth, but even when there is no clothing, the sex is not shown.

A clear desire for realism in representing the human body, and even a delight in showing its contours, characterises almost all of them. This trait is scarcely ever found in the other arts of Mesoamerica. In other contexts the figure becomes much more hieratic and loses its life-like quality. Perhaps this is because in later times it was almost always gods or priests—occasionally warriors—who were depicted, so that symbolism became more important than the figure. That is to say, the interest of the sculptor was focused on the adornments and elements which characterised the deity or denoted the rank of the personage, rather than on the physical aspect of the man.

This sculpture from Misantla still belongs to the great period of Olmec art, though it probably dates from as late as the fourth century B.C.

ALTAR
FROM LA VENTA
Plate 4

Even more massive than the heads are the rectangular stones which we call altars, another Olmec achievement. Relatively abundant, they are also very similar one to another. This altar from La Venta shows a jaguar in frontal view. We see the eyes, the open mouth with two large canine teeth between which appears an X—a symbol associated with the feline and basic to Olmec religion. Below there is a niche which may symbolise the animal's open jaws, containing a seated figure, whose tall headdress, necklace and jewels show that he is a person of importance. One hand rests on his instep while the other holds a cord which is tied to the neck of an individual—prisoner?—who appears seated on the side face of the altar. We have not been able to establish the symbolic meaning of this scene, which is repeated on other altars where the person seated in the niche or feline mouth has a child in his arms, a child who is dead in some cases and very much alive in others. It is probable that these altars served as a place to put offerings intended to propitiate supernatural forces or to solicit divine aid.

Although the style changed, the practice of building altars was to continue through all stages of Mesoamerican art. Among the Maya in particular the altar was often placed facing a stela, showing a scene with hieroglyphs, thus forming a combination of both elements. In this later period individual gods more complex than those of the Olmecs are invoked. In some cases the stela carries only dates—that is, it measures time. The altar facing it would be used specifically for invoking this concept of time, which the Maya sanctified.

'DANZANTE'
FROM MONTE ALBÁN
Plate 5

The march towards civilisation in the Valley of Oaxaca began around 800 B.C. with the first human settlement in Monte Albán. Later on, towards the end of what is designated the Monte Albán I period, one of the most interesting buildings we know of was erected—the Temple of the Danzantes. Its vertical walls were covered with great stone slabs placed in horizontal rows. Each slab is engraved with a human figure shown in a contorted pose—hence the name of *Danzante*, meaning 'Dancer'. The general aspect of these figures—face with wide nose and thick lips, nude body, simple headdress—is reminiscent, although somewhat remotely, of the Olmec style. It may be assumed, therefore, that they are the result of Olmec influence on the culture—already quite rich—which had developed in Monte Albán.

Some of these figures are accompanied by hieroglyphs and numerals, which shows that writing was known in this region since very early times, prior to its appearance in the Metropolitan Olmec world. Indeed, as far as we know, it is at Monte Albán that writing appears for the first time; it may therefore have been invented by the predecessors of those Zapotecs who were later to live in this region.

OLMEC SCULPTURE
FROM PAJAPÁN
Plate 6

This monolith from San Martin Pajapán has all the characteristics of the great Olmec style: the typical face of these people with heavy cheeks and down-turned mouth, the bodily proportions, and the adornments. The large headdress includes a mask with the face of a humanised tiger displaying the typical cleft in its forehead, another reference to its feline nature.

This statue has a curious history. Before interest in such objects had developed, the piece was seen in 1897 by an engineer named Loya who was making a survey of the region. As he needed a base point for his measuring, he moved the monolith a short distance: in the process the arms and the bar which they held were broken off. A rough sketch, crude and inaccurate, is the only record we have of the piece as it was before the accident. Years later the expedition of Blom and La Farge rediscovered the sculpture, in its damaged state, and for the first time published a photograph of it. During all the years of great activity in the Olmec region when the major part of the monoliths were discovered, the sculpture from San Martin Pajapán, in its mutilated condition, was photographed, drawn—for example by Covarrubias—and reproduced many times, but always in the incomplete form. The Museum of the University of Veracruz recently decided to display the piece in its collection, and so the surrounding area was explored; and as a result, the fragment which had been broken off and lost years before was found. Now for the first time we can observe this sculpture in its complete, or nearly complete form, just as it was conceived by the Olmecs in their heyday.

OLMEC SCULPTURE
FROM LAS LIMAS
Plate 7

This Olmec priest or chief, carrying in his arms a tiger-faced child, would in any circumstances be an exceptional piece of sculpture. It bears one distinction, however, which to our knowledge no other Olmec sculpture can lay claim: the figure has been venerated as the Virgin Mary. A year or two ago the piece was found by children in a field and carried to the little town of Las Limas (actually more of a settlement than a town) on the banks of the Coatzacoalcos River. Their parents thereupon decided to place it on the family altar. The importance of the effigy soon grew, since to it was attributed the power to settle problems about boundaries of land belonging to the town. The figure was given a small blue silk cape, and on its head was placed a crown of red flowers. The veneration of the statue reached such heights that it came to replace the Virgin of Guadalupe which had formerly reigned on the rustic altar, adorned with paper ribbons. The villagers assumed that the new acquisition too was a Virgin with the Child in her arms. Certainly a strange fate for this sculpture which not only is not the Virgin, but is not even a woman! It is clear that it represents a man dressed in a loin-cloth, seated with legs crossed, and carrying in his arms, as if to display it, the child with a tiger-face. While the modelling of the adult is magnificent and once more demonstrates the store which the Olmecs set by the beauty of the human body, the child is little more than a bundle, seemingly tied up or even dead. As sculpture, the child is far inferior to the priest who is carrying him. The latter wears only a very simple headdress—a sort of cap—but on the face, shoulders and knees there is a series of incised motifs in purest Olmec style. These include four anthropomorphic masks, each one different, and all showing the head with a cleft in the form of a V, so typically Olmec; they are very similar to those found on small objects, such as *hachas* or breastplates. The carving also bears the X sign which is probably an esoteric rendering of the jaguar's spots, found also in other manifestations of this culture. Although smaller than the Olmec monoliths (it is only 55 cm. high), with its slant-eyes and down-turned mouth it represents the aesthetic ideal of these people. But here these features are less pronounced and the nose—aquiline and much narrower—is quite different from the wide flat noses of the colossal heads.

We have no way of precisely dating this piece since the find was not made under scientific conditions. Nevertheless, the style, the glyphs and the masks incised on the main figure, and the tiger attributes of the child's face, show the piece to belong to the great Olmec period. It was probably carved about the fourth century B.C.

The Classical Period: Teotihuacán
and Monte Albán

The demise of the Olmec world is not really an end but a beginning, the beginning of the Classic period during which a great civilisation was to arise in all the major areas of Mesoamerica. We shall deal briefly with only four main areas: the Highland valleys, the Valley of Oaxaca, Veracruz, and the Maya, touching on minor ones such as Guerrero or the Huasteca.

No other single city ever attained the size and importance of Teotihuacán in the central Mexican valley. There, a minor village that originated three centuries before Christ was to grow into the great metropolis whose history was a pattern for the destiny of Central Mexico. In Teotihuacán we have for the first time a real city with a large density of population, obvious differentiation of social classes, professional groups, a viable economy, and of course, as Olmec times had already seen, a great monumental art.

As early as the end of the first period the city occupied some 17 sq.km. and had around 30,000 inhabitants. During period II (50 B.C.–A.D. 150) nearly 45,000 people lived there and it spread over $22\frac{1}{2}$ sq.km. At the peak of its development, what we call period III (A.D. 150–350), the city was slightly smaller but far more crowded, since it must have had no less than 90,000 people. In its last phase (period IV), which ended about A.D. 650, some 60,000 inhabitants were occupying 20 sq.km.

Throughout its various phases the whole of Teotihuacán was more or less a built-up area, although in the characteristic manner of cities the great monuments, mainly religious ones, were crowded in the centre. In this instance the centre ran along a main avenue called the Street of the Dead, and an important intersecting thoroughfare. Certain groups of buildings formed large complexes of an exclusively religious nature, while others seem to have served

Plates 1, 8

civil purposes, such as those surrounding what was probably the market place. The two great pyramids, of the Sun and the Moon, are still standing; each has in front of it a large plaza which was surrounded by other pyramids with temples atop. The Plaza of the Sun, though with a larger pyramid, presents a less striking appearance today; the Plaza of the Moon, beautifully *Plate 9* proportioned and conveying a tremendous sense of security and of permanence, is certainly one of the greatest aesthetic achievements of ancient Mexico. Only the great Plaza at Monte Albán, to which we will come later on, can compare with it.

Around the great temples of the gods and what were probably houses for the head priests, large sectors of the city were occupied by the palaces of the nobility. They are rather complicated affairs with many rooms and courtyards and passageways built in stone, stuccoed all over, and in very many instances painted with frescoes. It is here for the most part that nearly 200 ancient paintings were recovered. Farther from the centre, minor houses, probably those of artisans or small merchants, or of the people who made the innumerable objects which the archaeologists have recovered, were surrounded on the periphery by houses of the field labourers and the clans who actually tilled the fields and provided Teotihuacán with one of its economic props.

Teotihuacán architects invented techniques of building and a shape for the platforms and temples that were from then on to become the pattern of northern Mesoamerican architecture. Future peoples—the Toltecs and the Aztecs among them—were to change the proportions between the slopes and the panels slightly, sometimes to make larger or smaller staircases, or to top a pyramid with two temples instead of one; but the basic lines were determined and seem never to have changed. The influence of Teotihuacán architecture reached both Oaxaca and Veracruz, so that from then on every single temple built over a pyramid followed the pattern Teotihuacán had set.

Stone, usually simple, sometimes beautifully carved, is the basic material. In every instance it was covered with a coating of stucco and then painted in brilliant colours. The grey or brown ruins which we see today, monochrome and with the stone everywhere visible, are no more than the skeleton of what once existed.

On the other hand, the sculptors at Teotihuacán—no matter how wonderful some of their successes—never reached the heights to which Olmec sculptors had aspired. The few statues in the round that we have from the great city are mostly huge blocks, rectangular in over-all shape and geometric in pattern. It is only in the carved façades of some monuments, such as that from the Temple of Quetzalcoatl and the one, now unfortunately lost, from the building partially overlying the Pyramid of the Sun, that their stonework reached a high degree of perfection. In the first instance, faces of serpents alternate along the panels with the faces of a god who has been mistakenly identified as Tlaloc.

The small-scale sculpture, usually in fine stone, is quite remarkable. We have only to recall the little alabaster tiger, today in the British Museum, or the one found recently in the excavations of the city and now in the National Museum of Anthropology in Mexico, or the famous funerary masks, in order to appreciate the degree of perfection attained by the sculptors. *Plate 10* The masks are noble and simple. They do not portray violence or pain or joy but reflect a sense of immortality, with a view perhaps to imparting it to the body of the dead man over whose face they were placed. They are fashioned with a very sure hand; nature has been carefully observed even if idealised; sometimes these stone faces are quite lifelike, especially the masks with eyes of shell and obsidian.

The paintings too are arresting, as well as abundant. They can be classified in different groups according to the subject and the way it is treated. Thus some represent priests or gods in *Plate 11* ceremonial attire, frequently casting to earth their gifts to humanity. In another group animals are depicted—animals of all sorts, both real and legendary. There is too a type of painting that verges on the abstract; in it neither men and animals nor concrete objects appear, merely shapes created by the imagination of the artist. They may have been comprehensible at the time but it is impossible for us to understand them today. Some probably had no particular meaning but were simply decorative motifs, ornaments that were placed as a frame around the principal painting or in some cases, as in the Temple of the Quetzalpapalotl, were self-contained designs.

In addition to these frescoes—religious, of animals, or abstract—we have some examples that are far more descriptive; realistic, not necessarily as to their form, but because in them the artists sought to represent a real scene or rather, something they believed to be real. Two examples are particularly striking: the one of the offering to the gods, and the 'Tlalocan' at Tepantitla—a borough of the city. The first, unfortunately now lost, shows a temple on each side. In between there are at least twelve figures standing, seated, or in other positions, apparently dedicated to offering objects to the respective temples: thus one carries in his hands a dove and a pot, another a bowl of incense decorated with green feathers, and yet another small objects resembling tortillas. The dresses are quite remarkable and all different, many of a type that is not to be found anywhere else and which certainly did not survive into later times.

But the fresco at Tepantitla is still more important. It represents the paradise of the God of Rain. Only certain people could attain to it—not on their merits but through the manner of their dying. Those who had died by drowning or as a consequence of the numerous illnesses which were thought to be produced by water or themselves to produce water, went to the Tlalocan. Thus the word 'paradise' is rather misleading since there is no suggestion of a reward; the qualification is simply a fortuitous manner of death. The whole composition is divided into two parts, one on either side of the door. At the top, above both panels, a great figure of the God of Rain, sumptuously dressed, casts drops of water to earth. This is little more than another instance of the official paintings of the great gods. But the lower panels are far more interesting. To the right there is a mountain out of which runs a great river. The mountain itself is all water. What could be richer, what more desirable than a mountain of water? Both on the mountain and in the river men are swimming amongst fishes, plants and water animals. On the ground numerous little figurines, all masculine, are playing, talking or singing, chasing butterflies among the trees, the fruits and the flowers.

I think an important fact about this painting is that it gives us at least an inkling of Teoti- huacán philosophy, the philosophy of a people now defunct who left nothing in writing to provide a firmer basis. The Teotihuacán artist in representing paradise shows us what he thinks is the perfect life, a place of happiness where all the beautiful things in this world come together. Even the stones are of jade. Yet not a single woman is represented and there is apparently not the smallest interest in the beauty of the human body. How different from the Greek heavens peopled with beautiful men and women; how different also from the paradise of Islam! The houris, the cushions, the fountains, the perfumes, the sexual delights are entirely unknown in Teotihuacán's paradise. It is a simple heaven of almost childish pleasures, of games, of little boys. Really, the central theme is the richness of nature, a richness that produces water, the scarcity of which has been the nightmare of the Mexican Highlands from time immemorial; water that will seep into the dry land and make it fertile far more efficiently than all the sweat that men in the fields can pour into it.

In effect the crops of the Highland valleys could not have sustained this large city for nearly a thousand years, especially since so many of the people did not devote themselves directly to agriculture but to the production of those innumerable objects and luxuries we associate with Teotihuacán. Other sources, other ways of obtaining food for the population and certain materials unknown in the area must clearly have existed. These other sources quite obviously were the same as in the case of the Olmecs: war, tribute and commerce.

Around Teotihuacán itself there is a large area which we can call metropolitan since all the archaeological remains there are very similar to the ones found in the city. It includes at the least the valleys of Mexico and Puebla. Beyond it—in Oaxaca, in Veracruz, in Guatemala— at certain stages the influence or the impact of Teotihuacán is quite apparent. Certainly there were relations between all these areas, exports and imports were exchanged; but it is evident that foreign elements were introduced into the local patterns. This is unlikely to have resulted simply from pacific commerce. In many instances there are indications that a tribute was exacted, just as was to happen later in the Aztec Empire. In other instances all these factors probably played their part, as we have already seen in the case of the Olmecs. Then there is also the religious significance of a great city that was certainly a centre of pilgrimage and therefore a centre on which numerous people converged from different parts. The excavations at Teotihuacán have uncovered objects that came from all the major areas, thus showing that there was a widespread exchange of goods.

It is hard to say what political shape this took. Was Teotihuacán the hub of an empire and the other areas—or rather parts of the other areas—subjected provinces? Or was it more a question of various nations with the same basic culture but relatively independent of each other? At certain times Teotihuacán soldiers may have occupied, or at least partially conquered a province for the exaction of tribute. This does not necessarily mean that the conqueror would stay in the defeated province; for, once the area had been subjected he would set up a government friendly to him, impose a tribute to be paid at fixed dates, and return home. Merchants who were also soldiers would come on those fixed dates, collect the tribute and take it back to the capital. This seems to have been the system employed by the Aztec Empire, and very possibly was also the pattern in Teotihuacán times; at the same time the religious influence that we have mentioned

was clearly an important factor.

Actually the gods of Teotihuacán are to be found almost everywhere. It would appear that all through Mesoamerican history the same gods, with local minor differences, were worshipped in all the areas: the God of Rain, whom we have mentioned; Quetzalcoatl, the God of Wind and of Cultivation, a more or less friendly deity; and innumerable others, such as the quetzal and the combinations of various animals. It is only the guise that varies, modified by the   *Plates 12, 13* local style; but these variations are so slight that even today, with our little knowledge, we can recognise that we are dealing with the same deity whether he appears in Teotihuacán or in the Valley of Oaxaca or in the flat lands of Veracruz, or even as far away as the Highlands of Guatemala or the northern Petén. This is of course only partially due to direct Teotihuacán influence; it owes more to the fact that each area is simply a local manifestation of the same civilisation, to which the religious community forms the background.

Teotihuacán having disappeared towards A.D. 650, the later peoples, particularly the Aztecs of the fourteenth and fifteenth centuries, knew nothing of its history, but they were awed by the immensity of the ruins, so huge and so mighty that they could not believe that the city could have been built by man. They supposed it to be the work of giants and that the gods had lived and been created in Teotihuacán. From here stem most of the basic myths of Indian theogony. It was believed, moreover, that in Teotihuacán, through the sacrifice of the gods themselves, the Fifth Sun was created. The sun of course is essential to the world; it gives light and heat, it makes man and plants grow, it is life itself. Without the sun nothing endures, nothing can live. To the Indian mentality the sun is not a lasting phenomenon, but may be destroyed at any time; it must fight each night for its life, and at the end of every cycle it might disappear. Thus at least four suns had died already. At such critical moments the world was in darkness. The gods assembled and decided that a new sun must be created so that life would start anew and they would have men to worship them. The gods entered the fire they had built and one of them came out as a new and resplendent sun. This took place in Teotihuacán. The important thing about the myth is that it shows clearly the immense prestige of this ruined city in the Indian mind. Moctezuma himself, the last Aztec Emperor before the conquest, went yearly on a pilgrimage to Teotihuacán to render homage to the unknown gods, to those gods who though they belonged to the past were still fundamental for his religion and who have saved the world from darkness.

We have already dealt with the beginnings of civilisation in the Valley of Oaxaca. The advent of the Classic period there is marked by the spread of Teotihuacán influence; not only the pottery shapes and the wall paintings show this trend, but also the new architecture. The latter, directly derived from Teotihuacán, uses the slope and panel design; but it is far more than a variant, let alone a copy. It is an architecture of local inspiration even if it has borrowed the elements from elsewhere. Thus, the vertical panels of the temples in Monte Albán run uninterruptedly round the entire building, whereas in Teotihuacán each one is closed at the corners to form a complete frame.

The earlier inhabitants of the Valley of Oaxaca have already been mentioned as forming part of the Olmec world. During the Classic period they can already be referred to as Zapotecs since we know that from then on these people lived there, just as they still do today. If the Zapotecs did not actually invent their architecture but only modified and adapted alien forms, they were certainly, at least in Monte Albán and probably in many other still unexcavated sites, among the most extraordinary architects of Mesoamerica.

Monte Albán, the major site and the only one to provide us with direct evidence, was built on top of a group of mountains, about 500 metres above the Valley of Oaxaca. Not only *Plate 14* is the view superb but in their design the main plaza and the buildings that surround it are certainly to be counted among the masterpieces of Mesoamerican architecture. Today the stucco and the paint with which the stone-work was covered and the temples on top of the pyramids have all disappeared, but the splendid symmetry remains, the perfect proportions, the sense of perfection and permanence that only rarely is to be found anywhere in the world. To the people in the valley it must have been the centre of the world, the place nearest to the gods, where the great priests and nobles lived, the place to which they turned in prayer and supplication, the perfect fulfilment of their religious beliefs and of their desire for eternal life.

While in Teotihuacán the dead were cremated or buried in a very simple fashion, in Monte Albán the burial rites were far more elaborate; a tremendous complex of tombs resulted. As early as the very first period these tombs were made of stone with flat stone roofs. Gradually they become larger, more intricate, sometimes with two chambers, niches in the wall, and angular roofs. By the time of the Classic they are positively sumptuous. An elaborate façade was built even if it was destined to be covered immediately after the interment. The body of the deceased was laid in the centre of the tomb in an extended position and surrounded by numerous objects; a large slab, frequently covered with hieroglyphs, was used to seal the entrance. This attaching of importance to burial rites is of course not peculiar to the Zapotecs, but here we find it given exceptional emphasis.

Some of the tombs were even adorned with murals, which in certain instances recall the Teotihuacán frescoes. Here again, as in the architecture, the style is quite different though the similarities are abundant and easy to detect. In these paintings too, the priests are attired like gods; sometimes hieroglyphs indicate their names or their status. Nevertheless there is no indication whatever as to who was buried in these elaborate tombs; like all Mesoamerican art, they are entirely anonymous. There is not a single instance, even in the famous tomb at Palenque, where the name of the deceased or some inscription relating to him can be found. Our custom of putting the name of the departed on funerary monuments is entirely foreign to Mesoamerican ideas, as is the practice of the artist signing his work.

The Zapotecs' excessive preoccupation with the after-life is apparent not only in the tombs and in the care lavished upon the burials, but in the fantastic number of deities that appear in their pantheon. Were we to make a list of the many gods of Teotihuacán, and of the still more numerous Maya gods, neither would begin to compare in length with the roll of Zapotec gods. The famous urns—a characteristic feature of this culture—always represent some god or *Plates 15, 16* other, so clearly that even we can recnogise him. All the same, the confusion common to all mythologies is here enormous; thus combinations occur in which traits of one deity are mixed with those of another, forming a third. The difficulty lies in correlating the clearly distinguished sculptures with the deities mentioned in sixteenth-century accounts. In such cases we refer to each group of urns by a modern name.

These urns are perhaps the best example we can find of the evolution of Zapotec art from the beginnings of the Classic period to its end in the sixteenth century. At first the faces are rather realistic, frequently very beautiful. The adornments and the attributes necessary to show which deity is intended are soberly and meticulously wrought. But then gradually the style deteriorates, the ancient simplicity disappears, the decoration on the urns grows profuse, until it assumes more importance than the god himself. The faces become standardised, made in moulds and wholly lacking any life-like qualities.

Perhaps the fundamental difference between the Zapotec culture and that of Teotihuacán is that while the latter was always seeking to expand and continuously penetrating other areas for trade or for war, the Zapotecs seem to have been quite happy in their valley and the other areas they occupied. There was no urge to spread beyond their own environs; they simply received impulses from outside and adapted them to their own purposes. This applies particularly to the second part of the Classic period; once Teotihuacán influence had been entirely absorbed and perhaps even after the great city of the Highlands had disappeared, the Valley of Oaxaca seems to have built a wall around itself and to have run its course independently of all other places.

All this leads us to think that the Zapotec state was never an empire; also that it may have been far more theocratic than any of its neighbours. The great importance attached to funerary rites, to death, to the after-world and to the gods points to a priest-led society. Of course ceremonialism was prevalent in all of Mesoamerica, but in the Zapotec world it seems to have been more pronounced, enabling us to think in terms of a real theocracy. Theocracies, as we know from many other places in the world, do not seek to expand; they tend to be conservative and self-contained.

With the fall of Teotihuacán and with the increasingly introspective attitude of Zapotec culture, other peoples in the general region of Oaxaca began to emerge, people who must have been living there before but had not produced a culture sufficiently striking or sufficiently independent for us to distinguish it clearly. Things appear to have begun to change between 650 and 700. Of these emerging peoples by far the most important were the Mixtecs. But to them we shall return later, when we discuss the last great period of Mesoamerican history.

Monte Albán itself seems to have entered a period of decadence around the end of the ninth century or the beginning of the tenth. Gradually the city was abandoned, the great temples fell, the pyramids themselves started to disintegrate. People still lived on the slopes and certainly the ancient city preserved its prestige, but it was no longer the capital of the valley. Other cities took its place, although none ever became so glorious. Whether this slow decay of Monte Albán was due to internal difficulties, to a lack of understanding between the theocracy and the people, or whether external factors played their part, we cannot tell. We must remember, however, that the eclipse of Monte Albán coincided with the rise of the new peoples, heirs to the ancient cultures and represented in Central Mexico mainly by the Toltecs and the Mixtecs.

PYRAMID OF THE MOON. TEOTIHUACAN. Plate 8

PYRAMID OF THE MOON,
TEOTIHUACÁN
Plate 8

To the north of the great Plaza of the Moon in Teotihuacán stands the pyramid itself. Though it is smaller than that of the Sun, the god whose temple adorned the top must nevertheless have been very important, since the so-called Street of the Dead serves only as an avenue of access to the Pyramid of the Moon. 'Street of the Dead' is a double misnomer, for there are no burials along it or in the buildings which border it, nor is it really a street at all; it is made up of a succession of long plazas separated by stairways. For a society without wheels or draft animals, this solution was much more convenient and aesthetically more satisfying than would have been a real street. It allowed empty spaces to be delineated and the masses of buildings to be combined more harmoniously. Sometimes one of the latter stands in the middle of a plaza.

The pyramid itself—recently restored as far as reliable data allowed, i.e., up to the top of the third section—gives little idea of its original splendour, though we can appreciate its vast size. On the other hand the large extension at the front—once a feature also of the Pyramid of the Sun—remains almost complete today. Its five sections formed by *talud* (slope, or batter) and *tablero* (panel), in the manner invented at Teotihuacán, was to serve as the model for many later constructions. The low balustrade of the enormous staircase—which contains many of the original stones—has a rectangular projection on the level of the upper ledge of each section. If in imagination we add the stucco—of which only fragments remain—and the paint which is missing, the whole gives a very clear idea of what this great building was like in its prime.

GENERAL VIEW
OF TEOTIHUACÁN
Plate 9

No other city of ancient America can compare in size or importance with Teotihuacán. This view of some of the pyramids in the centre of the city in its last days of grandeur was taken from the Pyramid of the Moon, looking south along the great central avenue or Street of the Dead. The massive foundations of the temples, as if in order of battle, still show a splendid sense of urban planning, although the sanctuaries themselves have disappeared. In the middle distance to the left rises the enormous mass of the Pyramid of the Sun; its present form, due to a reconstruction made sixty years ago, is however not accurate. The plaza in front of the Pyramid of the Moon, with its adoratory, or place of worship, in the centre, is surrounded by twelve symmetrical buildings similar in height and size, which give it harmony and a rigorous classic style. The same elements are repeated on each of these buildings with their stepped construction. Each also has its staircase with low balustrade.

Originally the city limits reached the hills which are seen in the background. As a large part has not yet been excavated, we might think that vast open areas surrounded the monuments. This is not so. There were structures everywhere, and those gaps which we see today were occupied by palaces of the nobility and innumerable houses of craftsmen and other people. Their lower height makes them less noticeable, but any part of the ancient city proves a mine of objects and information as soon as the archaeologist starts digging. On the other hand, the great pyramidal foundations, which in their time supported temples of the gods, have always remained visible even though much havoc was caused by time and man's destructive urge. A few years ago they were rebuilt with great care. The result is fairly exact since enough data remained from which to deduce their original forms.

STONE MASK
FROM TEOTIHUACÁN
Plate 10

Teotihuacán is such a rich site that even a minor exploration yields an astonishing quantity and variety of small objects. They are mostly ceramic, but other materials, such as stone, bone, and shell are also found. Perishable materials have long since disappeared. There is an important collection of funerary masks carved from different types of stone. They are highly characteristic of the culture of this great city and represent perhaps better than any other minor objects the classic sense of harmony which is the very essence of Teotihuacán. These serene faces remind one of Baudelaire's definition of beauty: 'Je haïs le mouvement qui déplace les lignes et jamais je ne pleure et jamais je ne ris.' They not only have an austere simplicity but suggest the fundamental nature of the culture which produced them—an imperial world which fears no one and is not to be provoked, because it feels secure and superior to everything else.

Considering their material and their thickness, the masks could not have been used by living people. They were placed on the dead, or rather on the bundle which contained the corpse, wrapped in cloth. This was then burned—a custom disastrous for the archaeologist.

The making of stone masks had begun with the Olmecs, but they were given a new meaning by the Teotihuacanos. From this time on they were produced in the Central Plateau. Thus we have Toltec and Aztec masks, sometimes very beautiful, and obviously successors to those of Teotihuacán.

FRESCO REPRESENTING TLALOC
FROM TETITLA,
TEOTIHUACÁN
Plate 11

Many mural frescoes have been found at Teotihuacán. In the majority of cases these are true frescoes painted on damp stucco; therefore time has not caused excessive deterioration of the pigments. When in the course of an excavation a fresco emerges from the damp earth, each colour preserves its individual tone in harmony with the others, showing that no one colour has suffered more change than the rest. All the colours are of inorganic origin but were mixed with a rather thick agglutinate made of an organic substance. Sometimes iron pyrites was added and the tiny particles reflect the light, causing a special effect which is also used by some modern painters. There was not a great variety of colours at Teotihuacán, since the earth does not produce the necessary substances, but those that existed were frequently mixed with white before application, and in this way a series of different tones was obtained.

The larger compositions have clearly defined sections, a feature so characteristic and indeed essential in fresco work, since no matter how rapidly the artist paints, he cannot cover a large area in the brief time before the stucco dries. The wall must therefore be divided into sections, with plaster applied only to an area which can be painted before it dries. The indigenous murals were probably not done by one painter alone, but rather by a team. The master sketched the outlines, sometimes with a black line, while others filled in the spaces with the colours indicated.

Although greatly varied as to form and subject-matter, certain general themes are frequently repeated at Teotihuacán. Two of the most characteristic are sacred animals and gods in ceremonial attire. Our plate shows an example of the latter. Found at Tetitla, a suburb of Teotihuacán, it shows a god in all his splendour. Over his face he wears a jade mask, and above this an enormous rectangular headdress with the face of a quetzal in the centre. The bird's plumes are shown above and at the sides. The body of the god is covered with necklaces and adornments and from his open hands come jade objects which are falling to the earth, blue-green jade being associated with water because of its colour.

PILLARS IN THE TEMPLE OF
QUETZALPAPALOTL,
TEOTIHUACÁN
Plate 12

After the pillage and fire which demolished the centre of Teotihuacán in the fourth century, not a single roof remained in place; at the same time or perhaps later, almost all the walls of the temple and palaces also crumbled, leaving only low partitions. Therefore we have no buildings which are complete; nor can they be correctly reconstructed because it is impossible to know the original height of the walls, the form of the roofs, and numerous other such details. For this reason, when, during exploration of a palace in the south-west angle of the Plaza of the Moon, an opportunity of gathering such information was provided, it was an occasion for rejoicing. The central part of this priestly residence is an open patio surrounded by corridors. The roof over these is supported by columns carved in low relief. Although these columns were found in a thousand fragments, a precise reconstruction was possible: the individual pieces could be fitted together in only one way, and this enabled the height of the building to be ascertained. The floors still bore the imprint of the burned beams which had supported the roof. Thus it was possible to know what the roof was like.

During the reconstruction of this building it was discovered that on each of the four sides of each column the main motif is a mythological animal formed by a quetzal and a butterfly, i.e. the symbols of the Quetzalpapalotl in the Nahuatl language. The head of the bird, generally seen in profile, wears the characteristic plumes. Its body is formed in part by a stylisation of the butterfly—also typical—just as it is represented in many pieces of sculpture and in some pictographic codices.

BRAZIER FROM
TEOTIHUACÁN
Plate 13

It is not only in the Palace of Quetzalpapalotl that the bird with the marvellous green feathers appears as the central element—a sacred element. On many minor objects, among them some of the braziers so characteristic of Teotihuacán, we also find the quetzal. Numerous examples of these braziers have been found. The lower part is a vessel with a rim at the top into which fits an elaborately decorated lid. Such receptacles are used to hold fire; smoke comes out through a clay tube (not visible in the photograph because it is on the other side). It is the lid that is the interesting part. Crowning it is almost always a model of a temple. In the middle is the face of the god and around it, like two big wings, are his attributes. These wings represent the temple itself as if the god were looking out of the door, or in the more realistic cases, as if he were in the very back of the sanctuary. The whole was fashioned of small pieces of clay, each baked separately and then fastened to the lid and painted. That is why these braziers are so fragile and have always been found broken; in the case of the vessel here reproduced, however, all the fragments could be recovered and restored to their original position. Our plate also shows the centre of the quetzal's face with a dangling nose ornament over the beak.

The undeniably 'baroque' style of these braziers and their elaborate decoration—sometimes excessive—has led to the supposition that they belonged to the last period of Teotihuacán, when it was already in decline. This was not the case, since recent excavations have exposed them at levels which correspond to the great city's apogee.

MONTE ALBÁN:
THE PLAZA, FACING SOUTH
Plate 14

In the ninth century A.D. Monte Albán had reached the height of its splendour. It occupied the tops and sides of a group of hills situated where the three valleys meet which together form the Valley of Oaxaca. On the flat top of the Hill of Monte Albán, many centuries before, men had set about building one of the most astonishing plazas in America. First it was necessary to level vast areas—the entire plaza measures 600 metres from north to south, and 400 metres from east to west. At the northern and southern ends two hills, too large to be removed, were converted into foundations for temples, their sides being covered with *taludes* and *tableros* (see note to plate 9). The same was done in the centre of the great plaza, where three large temples conceal the natural hill that lies beneath them. Thus a magnificent harmony and unity was achieved, which even the inclemencies of weather and the vandalism of man have not been able to spoil.

Our plate shows the plaza, facing south. In the foreground appears the sunken patio built over the northern platform, with the characteristic adoratory in the middle.

Even in its heyday, Monte Albán did not go in for adornment or profusion of detail as did the Maya cities. Like Teotihuacán, it preferred great sobriety, and to let the sun play on its long horizontal vistas, forming contrasts of light and shade. Thus the lines are not broken and the plaza still preserves the dignity of a great sanctuary and of a site favoured by the gods.

ZAPOTEC URN FROM
CUILAPÁN
Plate 15

From its beginnings, the culture of the Valley of Oaxaca, represented mainly but not exclusively by Monte Albán, produced an abundance of urns which bear a human figure on the front. This feature, the most characteristic of the region, is to be traced throughout its entire history. Despite the changes imposed by time or caused by external influences, from the pre-Zapotecs of Monte Albán I until the days of the Spanish conquest these figures continued to be modelled in clay. Usually, and especially in the Classic and Late Periods, they represent gods, both masculine and feminine, progressively more elaborate and complex, becoming at the end almost a mass production of figures.

This urn from Cuilapán corresponds to Period II of Monte Albán and can be dated around the first century B.C. The figure is seated in the traditional pose with hands resting on crossed legs. Its nude body, with no sex shown, and its face still recall the Olmec style. Both on the tall headdress and on the breast a hieroglyph and numerals are incised. The upper hieroglyph perhaps represents water; the three dots are units, and each bar stands for five. The total should be read as thirteen. The hieroglyph on the breast, although it is accompanied by the same numerals, is different and difficult to interpret. It has been given the provisional name of the Q glyph.

ZAPOTEC URN
FROM MONTE ALBÁN
Plate 16

During Period III A of Monte Albán, between the second and fifth centuries A.D., the Zapotec urns possess all the characteristics of this Classic period. More than thirty deities—of which seven are feminine—are represented on these effigy vessels. They have a sober style with simple lines, at times conventional and showing little creative fantasy. The same motifs are frequently repeated but they are always executed with elegance and technical perfection. It is a highly professional art. The serene and realistic faces on the urns—even today similar faces can be seen in Oaxaca —are almost always very beautiful and well balanced. The adornment is not excessive, only enough to indicate—in an effective manner—the deity in question. The urn here reproduced represents a goddess, as the lavishly decorated skirt she wears shows. In this case the hands do not rest on the legs in the characteristic position, but are slightly lifted. Perhaps some object (flowers, feathers?) were placed in the hole formed between the thumb and fingers. A double string of jade beads with pendants adorns the breast.

The face is typical of the art of this period: it is in repose with the mouth half-open, and protruding lids above rather narrow eyes. At the sides great ear-plugs, also of jade, adorn the ears.

But it is the headdress which clearly indicates that this is a divine being. She wears on her head a tiger mask; we see the upper jaw, the nose and eyes of the feline. Above this emerges another mask, in this case a bird with a long half-opened beak. Above the bird is a further headdress formed by a central plaque—unfortunately incomplete—with two similar plaques at its sides. All this is within a curved element which represents a vessel, i.e., a container, indicating that the whole is a hieroglyph. Behind is a large plume of feathers.

The construction is somewhat like that of the Teotihuacán braziers (see Plate 13), with small pieces modelled separately and joined together before the final firing of the vessel. As the colours were applied after the piece was fired, they are not permanent. This example is one of the few in which the colours are conserved, although in pale tones.

The World of the Maya

Between the Isthmus of Tehuantepec and the southern border of Mesoamerica there are some 300,000 square kilometres inhabited by a variety of peoples speaking one or other version of the Maya tongue. Topographically, this vast area is very diverse, and at least two clearly defined geographical units can be distinguished. The Highland zone comprises the highlands of Chiapas and Guatemala and to it must be added the Pacific coastal region. The very different Lowland zone comprises the extensive densely wooded plain of the Petén and of the areas along the Usumacinta, the Grijalva, and the Motagua Rivers. Copán at one end and Palenque at the other mark its limits. The Yucatán Peninsula, which forms a northerly extension of this zone, is mainly a semi-arid region almost entirely flat.

Though we know little of the early history of its inhabitants, by the time the Olmecs had reached their heyday the beginnings of civilisation were already apparent in the various areas of the Maya realm. There are clear indications that this incipient Maya civilisation acquired a number of Olmec traits, while at the same time evolving its own pattern of living; like Monte Albán, it did not simply absorb Olmec culture, but combined ideas of its own with those it imported from southern Veracruz. This importation, moreover, does not seem to have been a direct process, but to have taken separate routes; one towards the Petén and the other towards Chiapas and the Highlands of Guatemala.

Thus we find, for instance, that one of the earliest great pyramids uncovered in the Maya area, the temple E-VII-Sub at Uaxactun, is decorated with large masks of jaguars, some of which look very much like the jaguar mask of the Olmec culture. But in Uaxactun they are made of stucco, a material unknown in Olmec work. The same thing is true of the stela and altar complex. Along the coast of Chiapas there are several sites—that of Izapa seems to be the most important—which represent a transition stage between the Olmec and the Classic Maya style. Some stelae at Izapa, in particular in association with altars, were to be adapted by the Classic Maya world and enormously enlarged to form one of its main features. The same thing is probably true of writing and calendrical inscriptions. It is likely that these also passed by way of other peoples into the Maya area, there to be developed to an extent unimagined by their original inventors.

It is difficult today to date the beginnings of Classic Maya culture. Whatever its dating—and this of course would definitely affect the dating for the Classic period in the Central Valleys of Mexico or in Oaxaca—Classic Maya is in large part contemporaneous with the Classic we have seen in other areas. This culture is so rich in content and reached such a high level of achievement, that only a very brief summary can here be given.

The Lowland Maya cities differ very markedly from Teotihuacán or the other cities of central Mexico. They show little over-all planning; none appears to have been as urban as Teotihuacán. That is why they are frequently considered to be no more than ceremonial centres featuring temples and palaces, which people would come to visit only for festivals, for markets or for business, while living in rather widely separated hamlets. Yet it is quite obvious that certain sites, for instance Tikal, the largest Maya centre, was, in fact, a city. It contained a planned centre with great pyramids and other monuments, surrounded by the houses of the different classes. All the same, even in the case of Tikal the planning is not as regular, as remarkably strict, as it was in Teotihuacán.

However we choose to name their centres, Maya buildings are usually arranged around plazas, on platforms or pyramids, in a rather regular pattern, but the Maya architect seems to have been more interested in the beauty of the façade and its adornment than in the relationship between one building and another. Perhaps this is the reason for the far more complex decoration —some of it wonderful, some of it excessive—which takes the place of vast empty spaces with their majestic austerity, or the alignment of the massed structures. The pyramids at Tikal in Guatemala are more than twenty storeys high; today still they emerge from the towering jungle like islands lost in a green sea. They are made of rock with earth filling the interstices and faced with limestone blocks beautifully cut and set with lime. Sometimes stone blocks

57

were used in true masonry style in the Petén, whereas in the Peninsula a veneer set in stucco is more usual. But Tikal and its like are exceptions; in most Maya monuments refinement is put

Plates 17–19

before size. For instance the famous Palenque temples are quite small and the same thing is true of the great majority, particularly in comparison with the immensity of Teotihuacán.

The palaces themselves, though much better built and far more permanent than those in the Highlands or in Oaxaca or Veracruz, have narrow rooms usually very few in number owing to the use of the well-known corbelled arch. This system of construction, very rare outside the Maya area, allowed for permanent roofs and a far more advanced type of architecture; on the other hand the vault restricts the size, since the Maya could never, not having known the true arch, overcome the strict limitations it imposes. Thick walls are necessary in order to sustain the vault, with the result that sometimes the wall is much thicker than the room itself. High over the roofs great comb-like affairs were erected parallel to the façades, giving even more height to the buildings. Although they have only a decorative purpose meant to enhance the importance of the temple, they help to balance the arches which must take the added weight. Roof combs occupy various positions, being most often in the centre or above the façade, thus giving the false impression that the monument, when seen from the front, is much higher than it actually is.

Temples are frequently set atop high pyramids while palaces are placed on lower and larger platforms. Some of these complexes—like that at Uxmal—have only one storey, but the

Plates 24–27

more typical ones of the northern peninsula, Kabáh, Labná and Sayil, are more elaborate affairs with three storeys. The rooms are not, in fact, placed one above the other but are stepped back from those on the lower level and rest on a compact fill. Thus terraces formed by the roofs of the lower rooms front the upper storeys.

Occasionally a vast rectangle is enclosed by four buildings, as exemplified by the famous

Plates 20–23

'Nunnery' at Uxmal. The façades facing this inner court are intricately carved with a profusion of motifs. As a rule the façade is formed by two bands divided by a moulding that runs all round the building. Mostly the lower band is left plain, the decoration being confined to the upper band. Thus in the great masterpieces of Maya architecture the façade is not over-ornate, but restful to the eye. We find the aesthetic counterparts of these façades on such European buildings

as the Palace of the Doges in Venice. Occasionally, it is true, mania for decoration went much

further and not a square inch was left empty. This applies also to some clay urns where the whole   *Plate 28*
surface has been covered with decorative motifs.

Another type of Maya structure is the great archway. Some of these stand alone like a triumphal arch; others form the entrance to a great court or complex of buildings. Here again, of course, we have not a true arch but a false one in which the same constructional device has been employed as for roofing. By comparison with this imposing architecture the houses of the people were probably small and simple, as they are today in the rural areas.

The sculpture of the Maya, remarkably fine and sensitive, can be divided into two main types: that which decorates façades or roof combs, and is part of the architecture, and that which takes the form of stelae and altars usually placed in front of buildings. The stelae are one of   *Plate 29*
the most important and best known features of Maya culture. Not only for their aesthetic value, but because on them were inscribed, beside human figures or just by themselves, long lists of hieroglyphs that have proved one of the greatest headaches for the archaeologists—and one of the greatest triumphs of Mayan intelligence.

The decipherment of Maya writing—now very much advanced, having made extraordinary strides since work on it was begun in the late nineteenth century—is still a matter of controversy and there are still many lacunae. Most progress has been made with the calendrical inscriptions, and in determining how the Maya reckoned time. As an Olmec heritage they had mastered the art of using a combination of signs (the equivalent of our digits) to build up multiple numbers. Why a day far back in the past was chosen as a starting point from which to reckon each subsequent day until their own times is still a mystery. For all Maya inscriptions known to us only start after the middle of the 8th Katun or cycle. Since each cycle represents 144,000 days, eight-and-a-half cycles constitute slightly more than 3,350 years reckoned from the beginning of mythological Maya history. This long span cannot in any way be equated with time as we reckon it, though some have attempted to do so. This initial date appears to be quite an arbitrary one, chosen probably for magical or religious reasons, and the actual counting of the days is likely to have begun much later.

The system is vigesimal and the numbers consist of dots for one and bars for five, plus a sign for zero. With these three elements a number of any magnitude could be inscribed. This system is usually known as the Long Count, as opposed to the one used by most other Mesoamerican peoples, which only included one small cycle of 52 years, after which the whole count would begin again; this has caused considerable confusion since it is almost impossible, except through archaeological digging or historical knowledge, to know to which cycle a particular date refers. This handicap is obviously not shared by the Maya Long Count. Unfortunately for us this was abandoned some time in the course of the tenth century (according to Correlation B). This means that the problem of correlating the Maya Long Count with the Christian calendar is a confusing business, since we have no information about it from the tenth to the sixteenth century. Many correlations have been proposed but the two most likely ones are: Correlation A, which places the beginning of the Classic Maya period around the first years of our era, and Correlation B, which makes it 260 years later. At the moment Correlation B is preferred, but there are strong arguments in favour of the earlier one. The earliest known Maya inscription yields the date 8.12.14.8.15 in the Maya calendar, the latest 10.4.0.0.0. (A.D. 292–909).

Maya painting is superb. Unfortunately, very few examples have survived. Far and away the most important are the frescoes painted in three rooms in a small temple at Bonampak. They depict a military expedition: the preparations for it, the battle, and the triumph. It is much nearer to our own concept of art: the way people are placed, the composition in general, the realism of many details, even the setting of some scenes—platforms or staircases against a real background of sky—shows a technique that differs greatly from that used in the famous Teotihuacán paintings. In the latter, realistic landscape is entirely unknown; trees or clouds have a magic function but not an aesthetic one. They also use the convention, frequently employed in the pictorial manuscripts, of painting part of an object to represent the whole. Thus, for example, the ears would symbolise a deer, the claw a jaguar, or the masks the god. In short, non-Mayan frescoes, whether they be great murals or not, are books; the painting is confused with the hieroglyph. Maya art at Bonampak is not like this. The composition is much more complex and advanced, although colours and technical procedure are the same or very nearly so. This great talent for painting is apparent even on the pottery. The few vases that have come down to us intact show the great potentialities of the Mayan painter. Some betray a humorous touch, indeed a rare phenomenon in Mesoamerican art!

All these arts and crafts seem to be the result of a social organisation which I believe to have been somewhat similar to that at Teotihuacán. A group of priests interested above all in ceremonial matters not only imposed its will on the population, but became the guiding force, forever thinking up ways of raising the standard of the community under its control.

In the Lowlands, however, political authority does not appear to have been exercised so effectively as in the Highlands, with the result that there was no over-all leadership to knit the whole Maya region into a unified empire. We should probably think, rather, of the Maya Lowland people as being divided into various provinces, with important links between them but each one more or less independent. That is why their styles, though fundamentally one, have many local characteristics that allow us to distinguish the products of one area from those of others.

Once again we find a world of peace and perfect harmony portrayed—for example at Bonampak—which reflects the aspirations of a people, a world of dream rather than of reality. For in actual fact there will have been war and destruction. One group will have grown strong and subjugated its weaker brethren. Much the same applied to the social order, where the hierarchy was certainly set far above the common people. The great tomb in the Temple of the Inscriptions at Palenque shows a burial in the pharaonic style of a man important enough to have a huge building erected for the sole purpose of housing a massive sarcophagus in which he had been placed with all his jewels, surrounded by the nine gods of death.

In the Mayan world again the power of the hierarchy was certainly based on knowledge. The influential men at the top were in a position to write and interpret the hieroglyphs and dates; it was they who could plan the buildings, the paintings and the sculpture; they were also the heads of state and the leaders. Nor is this at all surprising since, even allowing for the extent to which it deviated and the frequently higher level it achieved, the Maya Lowland world was clearly a Mesoamerican province and the basic aspects of its life and society were typically Mesoamerican; not only where the economy was concerned, which was more or less the same, but even in its religious approach. For a careful study shows that the Maya gods, though they had different names and were sometimes represented in a different way on aesthetic grounds, are fundamentally the same gods that we find in Teotihuacán or in Monte Albán or in any other place of Mesoamerica. That there was some degree of basic unity cannot be doubted, even if the Maya province was to a certain extent separated from the others and in many aspects excelled them.

Most of the more advanced features of Maya Lowland culture seem to have been absent from the Highlands: the corbelled arch, the stelae with inscriptions in the Long Count system, the carved façades, and much besides. None the less, it obviously fell within the Maya ambit. At Kaminaljuyu in the Guatemala Highlands there are signs of a strong Teotihuacán influence; so strong is it, indeed, that it has been suggested that a Teotihuacán group actually moved to Kaminaljuyu either during the heyday of Teotihuacán or after its collapse. Whether this is true or not, Mexican influences are prevalent both in this place and in many sites of the Pacific Coastal area.

The Classic culture along the Pacific Coast is still an enigma. Comparatively little excavation has taken place, the chronologies are still uncertain and it is almost impossible as yet to arrange the many objects and large monuments found there in any sound sequence. We do know, however, that the coast, an area geographically and culturally more remote from the Lowland than from the Highland Maya and frequently excluded from the Maya group, was at least in late times occupied by Maya-speaking people.

PALENQUE TEMPLE OF THE SUN. Plate 17

PALENQUE:
TEMPLE OF THE SUN
Plate 17

This small and charming monument rises from a much higher base than other near-by temples in Palenque. The base itself is 8 metres high, and the temple including the roof comb measures 11 metres. Each of the pillars of the façade contains a tablet showing a standing figure wearing large adornments and feathered head-dress. On the frieze there are stucco decorations, now unfortunately very damaged, which show a central seated figure flanked by two kneeling ones with a large mask below. Above the building rises the graceful roof comb formed by two parallel fretwork walls with a gap between them.

While the exterior is remarkable, the interior is even more so. It consists of two long parallel passages somewhat less than 3 metres wide and has three openings separated by two pillars. In the back is the sanctuary, a characteristic feature of the Maya temples of this region and which in reality forms a small temple inside the bigger one. The door jambs are also decorated with standing figures seen in profile and facing towards the doorway. They bear various hieroglyphs. On the back wall of the sanctuary is a large panel formed of three sections in the same style as those of the Temple of the Cross and the Temple of the Foliated Cross. Each of these panels is a masterpiece of Maya art. As they are carved in a rather soft chalky stone, the artist could achieve not only many details but a great refinement of line. A mask of the sun appears in the middle of the panel which adorns the Temple of the Sun, as if it were a coat of arms placed over two crossed lances, all this above an altar which is profusely decorated and distinctly 'baroque' in appearance. On each of the side panels stands a figure looking towards the mask of the Sun and with its feet planted on another figure prostrate on the ground. The standing figures carry manikin sceptres in their hands (see Plate 29). Completing the panels are four compact columns of hieroglyphs which show the date December 6, A.D. 642. Behind and at the foot of the Temple of the Cross flows a small river, the Ostolun, which was the source of the water supply for Palenque and part of which has an artificial bed excavated by the Maya.

PALENQUE:
PALACE, TEMPLE OF THE CROSS,
TEMPLE OF THE FOLIATED CROSS,
TEMPLE OF THE SUN
Plate 18

In June 1787 Captain Antonio del Rio made the first exploration of Palenque on behest of Charles IV of Spain. His report states that with 'seven small bars and three axes' he attacked the numerous buildings and 'by virtue of perseverance, I did all that was necessary in such a manner that at the end not one door or window remained sealed, there was not one dividing wall which was not torn down, not a single room, hallway, patio, tower or underground passage in which excavations of two or three varas in depth were not effected . . .'. One trembles on reading this paragraph. If it had been true, little would have remained of the splendid city. Happily, Antonio del Rio was grossly exaggerating and his destructive actions were not too serious.

This plate shows part of the ruins which have won the admiration of so many travellers; in the words of John Lloyd Stephens, when he beheld them in 1841: 'What we saw does not need any exaggeration. It awakened admiration and astonishment.' To the left, upon a low but very extensive mound, stands the Palace; the great staircases for access to it still exist but have not yet been uncovered. Should

the foundations ever be excavated, they will show that as in all great Maya palaces, the platform serves only to add height to the structure and thereby increase its impact on the viewer. From one of the interior patios of the palace rises a square tower of three storeys plus a mezzanine. This building, with its complex plan, interior staircases, and curious roof is unique in Mesoamerica. In the centre and to the right of the photograph are some of the better-known temples. The tallest is the Temple of the Cross; between it and the Temple of the Sun, the Temple of the Foliated Cross can just be discerned.

In the background we see part of the amphitheatre of hills which surrounds Palenque on three sides. Numerous minor buildings which have not yet been excavated are hidden by a dense and almost impenetrable jungle. On the fourth side a superb view is obtained over the vast plain of Tabasco, extending on clear days as far as the waters of the Gulf of Mexico.

PALENQUE:
TEMPLE OF THE CROSS
Plate 19

Although unfortunately in a bad state of preservation, the Temple of the Cross was originally very beautiful. It is quite similar to that of the Sun both in the exterior and interior design except that the former is a little bigger and its roof-comb is proportionately much taller. Not only has the architecture of the Temple of the Cross suffered a great deal, but most of its adornments have been lost and its tablets carried away. The two tablets appearing on either side of the entrance to the sanctuary had been moved before Stephens visited the site (1840), and placed in a house in the town of Santo Domingo de Palenque. The distinguished traveller wanted to buy the tablets, but as the owners refused to sell, he decided to buy the entire house, although this transaction was never carried through. The tablets are now displayed in the local church.

But even more curious is the history of the large panel formed of three tablets—like that of the Temple of the Sun—which was in the back of this sanctuary. Stephens relates that when he visited Palenque the tablet from the right side was broken into thousands of fragments, the central tablet had been moved from the site by some people who tried to carry it to the town but had left it lying on the ground, at the mercy of the elements, and only the third tablet—that to the left—remained *in situ*. The fragments of the right-hand tablet were collected and glued together by the Consul of the United States in Laguna and sent to the United States in 1842, finally being placed in the Smithsonian Institution. The central tablet was later brought to the National Museum of Mexico. Finally, in 1908, the Secretary of State of the United States ordered that the Smithsonian tablet be returned to Mexico, and the third, which was still in Palenque, was also transferred to the National Museum. Since then, the three parts again united, they form one of the most important possessions of what is now the National Museum of Anthropology.

The complete panel, like that of the Temple of the Sun, has long rows of hieroglyphs on both sides and two standing figures, also with large sceptres, facing the central element, but here this element is in the form of a cross—which gives the temple its name. Of course it is not really a cross but a tree drawn in the Maya fashion and placed over a large mask; on top of the tree stands a quetzal.

Uxmal:
Nunnery Quadrangle
Plate 20

The northern part of the Yucatán peninsula forms an enormous chalky plain, flat, hot, and with rather sparse vegetation. Towards the south-west—in the direction of Campeche—there is a slight rise in the land known as the Puuc, meaning Sierrita or Ridge of Hills; this would not stand out in the rugged landscape of Central Mexico, but in Yucatán it takes on the proportions of a mountain. In that region during the Classic period was elaborated an architectural style which was undoubtedly Maya and had many similarities to those of other regions inhabited by these people; but also had its own distinctive features, such as an extraordinary richness of decoration on its façades, and refinement in the sculptured motifs.

Surely the queen of the Puuc cities is Uxmal, not only because of its important history and the number of buildings it can boast, but for their quality and size. The magnificent complex shown in this plate is known as the Nunnery Quadrangle, although this name does not reflect the original use to which it was put. On each of the four sides of a vast patio measuring 65 by 45 metres and bordered by sidewalks there are buildings, known as the North Building, South Building, etc. They all have an exterior façade, but greater care has been lavished upon the one facing the patio, which must have been considered the more important. The entrance to the group is on the south side and is formed by a tall vault which reaches the height of the upper cornice. The rest of the façade—and this applies to all the buildings of the quadrangle—has the lower part plain and the upper part decorated, in this case with a stone grille-work on which reproductions of huts with roofs of straw—replaced here by rich adornments of feathers—are outstanding. Between the panels there are rows of slender columns. Both the East and the West Buildings are built upon a huge platform with a staircase at the front which extends the whole width of the façade. The decorations of the upper sections of the two buildings differ, but both have grille-work for a background and both are very sumptuous.

The records show that the Uxmal Nunnery was greatly admired by travellers for many centuries past. It is one of the rare indigenous buildings mentioned in the sixteenth century; Fray Alonzo Ponce, who visited Uxmal as early as 1588, was greatly impressed by the Quadrangle and devoted several pages of his *Relacion* to the complex, referring to it as 'superb buildings in a square'.

UXMAL:
NUNNERY QUADRANGLE,
DETAIL
Plate 21

This detail from Uxmal is a splendid example of one of the most characteristic architectural decorations of the Puuc style and also shows features of other styles we associate with the Maya world. I refer to the superposing of a simple element— masks of the Rain God—one above the other. We find this again more profusely used on the Codz Pop at Kabáh (see Plate 25). At Uxmal—more elegant in every respect—they never cover the entire façade but are grouped one above the other to form together an important decorative element. In this plate we see four masks which decorate a corner in the Nunnery Quadrangle (see Plate 20) and therefore appear in profile. They have the eye of the god, the nose-plug which must have been of jade, the mouth, and the long nose which protrudes from the building, the tip curled back. For each element the stones had to be carved to a special shape and then fitted together like a true mosaic. Once they have fallen apart, to reconstruct them is like working an immense jigsaw puzzle until one finds precisely which eye, which ear-plug, which mouth, fits each nose and each of the ornamental details. Of course this complicates the archaeologist's work, but if it is done with due care and the necessary skill we can be virtually certain that each piece has been restored to its original place.

The photograph shows the thick nucleus of rubble and lime which formed the walls, as well as the covering of finely carved blocks which are purely decorative and lend the architecture of Yucatán such an extraordinary distinction. On the other hand this utilisation of the faces of the gods simply to ornament its palaces gives the impression of a culture which—while not neglecting its religious principles— attaches more importance to the decorative aspect of these images than to their value as objects of veneration for the faithful.

UXMAL:
NORTH BUILDING OF
THE NUNNERY QUADRANGLE
Plate 22

The North Building of the Nunnery is the most important of the Quadrangle and stands higher than the others, since it was built over a platform almost 100 metres long and 7 metres high. Running up to the base of the building itself there is a great staircase (to the right in this photograph) which is 30 metres wide. At its side is what could be considered the first floor. As in the Palace at Sayil (see Plate 24), leading off this there is a series of rooms, their entrances separated by pillars.

Above the plain lower portion of the building proper is a wide, wonderfully ornamented border containing huge masks which extend above the flat roof of the building. These masks consist of superposed faces of the God of Rain. They alternate with models of huts over whose feather-roofs stylised two-headed snakes curl. Between these motifs appear frets or rhomboidal elements. Above the cornice, which slants slightly outward, are projecting masks, very interesting because they depict the God of Rain, not in his usual Maya form, but as he is represented in Central Mexico. The year-glyph done in the Teotihuacán style also occurs. This is one of many such proofs of the international character of Uxmal, a quality so typical of great Mesoamerican cities but rarely found in Yucatán before the arrival of the Toltecs. At Uxmal the characteristic Puuc style has combined with it elements—less clear but quite in evidence—of another style which is likewise Mayan, and partly contemporaneous; it is called Chenes after the south-eastern region of the Puuc Mountains.

Uxmal:
Governor's Palace
Plate 23

Among the many fine buildings in Uxmal, the Governor's Palace is outstanding; in my opinion it is one of the most beautiful monuments of America, and Eric Thompson has said that 'it is one of the most imposing buildings of the Maya area'. The palace stands upon a great platform with three levels connected by stairways, and consists of a large central body and two identical wings. The whole complex is 98 metres long, 12 metres deep, and 8·60 metres high. Roofed hallways with very high vaults—the tallest of the Maya world—connect the three sections, whereby it used to be possible to circle the central portion without going around the whole structure. The Maya later closed off these hallways, making small rooms out of them. All the doorways of the centre block are on the façade side, which means that the interior rooms do not receive direct light. Each of the two wings has an exit at the side.

If the proportions and size are noteworthy, the decoration on the upper part of the façade is remarkable. The lower part is again entirely plain, except for the moulding formed of sequences of little columns, yet this wealth of decoration above the level of the door jambs does not interrupt the unity and rhythm of the over-all design. For example, we find superposed on a stone quadrangle which serves only as a background, frets, serpent heads, and representations of huts. Of the five sculptured figures seated on a throne with an enormous, very rich canopy which completed the adornment, only one now remains.

SAYIL: PALACE
Plate 24

The second of the three Puuc palaces we include in this book is that of Sayil, near Kabáh. But in contrast to the other two, here the Uxmal spirit is again apparent, though there are many basic differences. In a bad state of preservation, the Sayil palace still reveals the great skill of the workmen—a feature of all Pucc architecture— and the remarkable talent of the architect—which is not in evidence at Kabáh (see Plate 25).

The palace has three storeys, in stepped formation, the upper ones being supported by a solid fill set back from the floor below. They are connected in front by a great stairway of three flights, allowing access to the terraces which result from this arrangement. The lower façade, rather plain, had only adornments of stucco or rows of little columns above the level of the doors. The middle storey is by far the most elaborate with its series of little columns on the moulding, between the doors and on the frieze. At the corners the characteristic masks are to be seen, while in the middle of each section a carved panel shows a god descending—a frequent figure in Mesoamerica—flanked by two serpents in outline. The third storey had above each of its seven doors (five at the front and one on each side) a human figure in stucco placed on a pedestal. The rest is completely plain. The whole structure is characterised by the desire for rich ornamentation contrasted with extensive plain surfaces. Not without justification do various scholars consider the Palace of Sayil to be one of the great triumphs of Maya art.

We do not know who built or inhabited this vast structure of seventy rooms. The city, like Labná and Kabáh, seems to have been abandoned before the arrival of Toltec influence in the tenth century A.D. There were no dated inscriptions here— or at least none have been found—but in neighbouring Puuc cities, the latest dates are all around the middle of the ninth century, except for Uxmal which has one giving the year 909.

KABÁH:
PALACE (CODZ-POP)
Plate 25

In the Puuc cities, whose monuments date from the seventh to the tenth centuries A.D., great changes were made in Mayan architecture. In contrast to the old walls built with blocks of stone, they are here constructed with a nucleus of rubble covered over with thin slabs of beautifully cut stone. Columns and stones specially shaped to support the vaults replaced interior walls, providing more space and light in the dark rooms. Not only this changed the appearance of the façades; the stucco previously used was replaced by true stone mosaics, each piece carved precisely to fit the corresponding space.

A short distance to the south of Uxmal are the ruins of another Puuc city, Kabáh. Less thoroughly explored than Uxmal and of less importance, it nevertheless has some very interesting buildings, the principal one being the palace called Codz-Pop. The name derives from the nose of a large mask which serves as a stepping stone between two interior rooms and which actually looks like a rolled-up mat. Although now mostly in ruins, enough remains to give us an idea of what it was like. In contrast to the Governor's Palace at Uxmal, the Codz-Pop has rooms on different levels and possibly was designed to have two storeys, one set back behind the other. But the second storey was never built; instead, upon the nucleus which had been prepared, an enormous roof comb was erected. Tatiana Proskouriakoff believes that perhaps after the façade was finished the builders were disappointed and decided to complete the structure in a simpler fashion than had originally been planned.

The decoration of the façade of the Codz-Pop is in fact overpowering. Row upon row of enormous masks cover every square foot of surface without leaving any scope for repose; and not only the front, but also the sides and perhaps the wall behind were covered with this very showy but overcrowded decoration. Such elaboration does not seem to conform with the sober and refined spirit of the Classic Maya. Perhaps this resulted from the particular social and political make-up of these Puuc cities, where frequently the palaces and residences—that is, dwellings for man— were more important than temples dedicated to gods.

LABNÁ: TEMPLE
Plate 26

Another city in the Puuc style is Labná, near Uxmal. Its most important building, although in a bad state of preservation, is the great palace. A long highway paved with stones leads from the palace towards the group of which the Mirador forms part. In the plate we see the Mirador—a name without any real significance—which stands atop a relatively tall pyramid. The front part of this temple is divided into three rooms, a central one flanked by two others. Behind the room in the middle and communicating with it is another, forming the sanctuary, all being roofed with the Maya vault. Although much simpler than those of Palenque, the façade also had its decoration, in the form of standing figures somewhat larger than natural size with a big ornamental motif in the middle. All the statues were placed on pedestals, but very little remains of these today.

A notable feature is the enormous roof comb more than 4 metres in height, which gives the temple a lofty and imposing appearance. Unlike those at Palenque, the comb is not placed on the transverse axis of the building but aligned with the façade, so that on viewing the building from the front it looks like a prolongation of the latter; and it consists of only a single wall. This type of roof comb placed in front, whilst it corresponds to the Classic Period, is characteristic of the Yucatán zone and not to the zone of the great rivers, as in Palenque.

Labná: Archway
Plate 27

In Yucatán the ever more frequent use of the Maya vault led to the erection of enormous vaulted doorways such as those of the Governor's Palace at Uxmal. In Kabáh this is carried even further, for at this site there is an almost independent Maya gateway which puts one in mind of the triumphal arch. This plate shows an arch of like monumental proportions at Labná, but it is not quite independent since it serves as a communicating doorway between two ceremonial patios. This huge ornamental gateway has a small roof comb above the main opening, as though it were a temple. The chambers on either side are in classic Puuc style: the lower part of the façade is entirely plain, while the upper part is decorated with the characteristic lattice pattern, with, in the middle, models of huts which perhaps formerly contained a piece of sculpture.

The much damaged building on the left has a façade decorated with multiple rows of columns so arranged as to suggest bamboo; perhaps it is this which gives the structure its vaguely Oriental look—providing one more argument in favour of those who claim some sort of connection between the two continents.

The outlying buildings at Labná are connected with the town by a cobbled street, similar to that running from Uxmal to Kabáh, which is to be found in many other sites of the Yucatán area. These well constructed and smooth-surfaced avenues, some of them very long, must have served some ceremonial purpose. For a people without draught animals and without the wheel, the immense labour of building such roadways across the peninsula would only seem justified if primarily intended for such use, rather than for transport of merchants and merchandise.

MAYAN URN FROM TEAPA
Plate 28

This magnificent urn, 60 cm. tall, can be dated to the second half of the eighth century A.D. Although known as the urn of Teapa—after the municipality in which it was found—its provenance is more precisely Ixtapanjoya, Tabasco, and it is now in the Museum of Villahermosa, Tabasco. At the back it takes the form of a crudely-fashioned vase, which contrasts with the carefully executed front part of the vessel; hence its classification as an urn.

The central figure is seated cross-legged on a throne, taking the form of an elaborate mask which perhaps represents the earth monster and therefore the Underworld. Like a canopy above the figure is a jaguar-head, from which emerges a plant or flower with a small human head among its petals. On either side is a little square resembling the transverse section of a marine conch shell, from which another human figure peers out. The sides are made up of a plant-like decoration, the stems seemingly supported by two further figures. All this has clear affinities with certain stelae of Yaxchilán, a site not far away, even with Copán in Honduras and with some types of Jaina figurines in Campeche. It is Maya art in full bloom, at times almost entirely 'baroque'. Indeed there are some stelae and other Mayan pieces of this period whose adornment is so profuse, that not a fraction of an inch is left undecorated. We know this *horror vacui* to have developed towards the end of the 'great period', and it is exemplified by this urn.

It has been suggested that the urn represents the voyage which the soul of the deceased makes, descending first to the Underworld, and later passing through various realms or heavens on its way to ultimate repose. Such a theme is characteristic of indigenous thought, although in this case the central figure is not shown with eyes closed, as is usual for representation of the dead.

CARVED MAYAN LINTEL
FROM YAXCHILÁN
Plate 29

Yaxchilán, situated on the banks of the Usumacinta River, is one of the great Classic Maya cities that have been little explored; but its importance is such that Sylvanus G. Morley believed it to have been the leading element in the aesthetic field of the Maya world at one time. There are numerous buildings at this site and a great many inscriptions in stone—on stelae, altars and lintels. The piece reproduced here is Lintel 43; now in the National Museum of Anthropology in Mexico City, it measures 1·20 metres in height. The lintel was, according to Morley, carved on February 6, A.D. 701 and originally adorned a doorway in the western acropolis of the city. It was discovered by Sir Alfred Maudsley in 1882; at that time already the large fragment, entailing most of a second figure, was missing from the left-hand side.

The intact figure shows a person of importance, richly attired and bejewelled, and wearing an enormous headdress of plumes. He carries a staff in his hand on top of which is seated a little figure of the god with the long nose. This suggests a manikin sceptre, an object which great Maya personages carried in their arms as a symbol of their exalted rank. Of the figure to the left there remain only the feet, the skirt, and the hands which hold a vessel containing a coiled snake. There are three groups of hieroglyphs (two above and one below), and the upper left-hand one indicates the date of the lintel. Because it is broken there could be some doubt about the date, but Morley's is almost certainly correct. The other inscriptions have not yet been deciphered.

These lintels and stelae are among the most characteristic and important works left to posterity by the Maya culture. They vary from the early stiff and simple designs to elaborate compositions full of meaning. This example is particularly beautiful because of the extreme fineness of the work—note the design in the skirt of the incomplete figure, and the minute details of the jewels worn by the other— its relatively high relief, and the skilful execution of the composition as a whole. Unfortunately these pieces of sculpture were only dated for a period of six centuries —approximately from A.D. 300 to 900—and after that such a perfect system of counting was abandoned. We therefore have difficulty now in correlating the Mayan dates on stelae with the Christian calendar.

The Gulf Coast Civilization: Tajín

The Veracruz area along the Gulf Coast is the least known of all. Although numerous sites have been discovered and it has yielded an important collection of objects, particularly of stone, it is still very difficult in the present state of our knowledge to determine the prevailing trends of that culture, or rather of the group of cultures that form the long coastal area from the ancient Olmec territory to the northern border of Mesoamerica.

Certain Olmec sites like Tres Zapotes and especially Cerro de las Mesas, continued to be occupied during the whole Classic period and even beyond it. At Cerro de las Mesas stelae inscribed in the Long Count system have been uncovered. This is perhaps the only case in which this system was used outside the Maya area.

Plate 30 But what appears to have been the centre or at least the most important site, Tajín, lies farther north; here, not only an enormous amount of construction took place but some of the *Plate 31* most interesting monuments of the Classic period have been found. The famous Pyramid of the Niches, though not unique in its style, is certainly the most representative and the most important building there. Among other temples or palaces found at Tajín, one had human figures carved *Plate 32* on its columns. The inhabitants were obsessed with the ball game; seven courts have been uncovered at this site. The largest has on either side of the field low reliefs in stone depicting ceremonies connected with the ball game; although far more ancient, it has much in common with the later version associated with Chichen Itzá.

Tajín seems also to have been the centre for, although probably not the originator of, *Plate 33* a number of objects that must have been in great demand, since they were traded all over Mesoamerica. They include curious yoke-shaped stones, beautifully carved and probably worn around the waist of the ball players. Also fairly common are stones, decorated with human or animal figures and the very intricate scrolls which seem to be the main characteristic of the Tajín style since they appear in practically all its products, small objects and monuments alike. Then there are the ceremonial axes, obviously not meant for practical use, whose blades are frequently shaped like a human head and more or less of that size, but cut in the shape of a triangle, so that they must be viewed in profile to see the facial characteristics. Other curious stones whose use is entirely unknown look like pieces of machinery. Finally—although these are perhaps slightly older—we must mention the well-known heads that are encountered at many Veracruz sites. The fact that their faces often seem to be grinning, an expression very rarely encountered in Mesoamerican art, lends them particular significance. Some of these elements may stem from the late pre-Classic, but they developed during the Classic period and probably even towards the end of it, since in certain places like Palenque they overlay the ruins of the Classic Maya.

These objects probably owe their wide distribution not only to trade but also to actual migration, perhaps of the peoples known as the Pipil, all the way to Central America. Unfortunately, we cannot relate any archaeological objects or sites to this elusive group. However, in the later chronicles the Pipil are frequently mentioned and their language spread as far as Panama. Their name signifies 'nobles' or 'princes', and they seem to some extent to have been heirs to Teotihuacán culture. After a good deal of moving around, they apparently settled for some time in the Veracruz area. Equally ubiquitous is the distinctive design of the Tajín scrolls (it has appeared as far away as in Teotihuacán and Kaminaljuyu), which is evidence not only of its appeal but the wide range of the traders or migrants who helped to spread it abroad.

Farther northwards the Huastecs had by this time evolved a clearly defined culture. Although Mesoamerican, the fact that it was adjacent to that of non-Mesoamerican peoples to the north gave it certain peculiarities and a foreign flavour. If the Tajín culture is still difficult to understand, the Huastec is far more so and until further excavation is done, little information can be given except for a physical description of its objects which include some marvellous stone sculpture.

Plates 34, 35

GENERAL VIEW OF TAJÍN
Plate 30

The central region of the present state of Veracruz where the Totonacs live is rich in archaeological monuments and other remains of numerous cultures. But it was in Tajín that the most important culture in this region originated in pre-conquest times. Located some 30 kilometres from the Gulf of Mexico and only slightly above sea level, it has a hot and humid climate. For this reason the site is surrounded by a dense jungle which for centuries concealed its monuments. Nothing was published about the principal pyramid, known as *Los Nichos* (the Niches), until 1785, and serious exploration of the zone began only in 1935. Since then work has been carried on there more or less continuously, but while a good number of buildings have already been uncovered, the majority, although cleared of vegetation, still await excavation. These appear as green mounds in the accompanying plate, which shows only part of the site. The great buildings which they conceal seem to be disposed around vast plazas, suggesting a sense of ordered urban planning on a huge scale. Although the history of Tajín extended over many centuries, its floruit was between A.D. 500 and 1200.

This photograph was taken from the so-called Little Tajín—an important group of monuments situated on a slightly higher level—and shows the Pyramid of the Niches (seen in greater detail in the next plate) and, beyond and to the left, Buildings I and V bordering the great plaza in front of it.

The tall pole to the left is used in the famous ceremony of the *Voladores* (Flying Dancers). Five men climb up to the very top of the pole. Four of them are attached to ropes which slowly unwind, and they descend to the ground in ever-widening circles; they are dressed like birds and try to imitate their flight. The fifth man stays on a very small platform at the top of the pole, dancing and playing an instrument. The game is highly spectacular although very dangerous, and like all Mesoamerican games, it has religious implications.

The architects of Tajín invented, or at least utilised, a number of very special constructional and decorative elements. For instance they were able to roof over large areas with a material resembling poured concrete. This they did in layers using lime and sand in combination with wood, fibres, pumice stone, and even potsherds to lighten the weight. They made much use of the niche to give articulation to exterior surfaces, and enormous serpentine frets run lengthwise along the façades. Sometimes Maya-style vaults appear, and of course the basic idea of the batter and panel, which suggest Teotihuacán influence.

Tajín:
PYRAMID OF THE NICHES
Plate 31

The famous Pyramid of the Niches is the best known monument at Tajín. Its base is 36 metres square and the whole structure, made up of storeys each set back from the one below, and a temple on top, of which almost nothing remains, is about 25 metres high. The terrace-like ledges resulting from this construction were not utilised since the great stairway does not have access to them. Each storey is made up of a base with the customary batter, supporting an extended panel topped by a projecting cornice. The panel, from which the building derives its character, is decorated not in the Teotihuacán or Monte Albán manner but with niches of varying depth. Contrary to popular belief, these niches were empty from the outset and are purely decorative, forming a play of chiaroscuro. Their interior was painted dark red and the frame was blue. There are niches not only in the visible parts of the monument, but also beneath the enormous stairway at the front. This points to the builders never having regarded the stairway as an integral part of the pyramid but rather as something superposed on it, like a garden ladder leaning against a wall. In the centre of the staircase there are five groups of three niches each, which do not correspond to those of the building proper; the wide balustrade on either side is adorned with thirteen frets in relief which are a stylisation of the body of the serpent. Since the niches, including those of the foundation of the temple, total 365, there is obviously a connection—as there was to be later in the case of the steps of the Castillo at Chichen Itzá—with the days of the year. Furthermore, the thirteen frets of the low balustrade of the staircase represent the days of the indigenous week. Also as in the Castillo at Chichen Itzá, there is an older pyramid, similarly proportioned, within the building we can see.

The stones in the foreground, facing the staircase, are the remains of a small quadrangular altar which was once adorned with little niches. In front of the pyramid are some stone cubes with holes in the centre, arranged symmetrically. These were probably used for holding flag poles, on the banners of which holiday celebrations were announced.

TAJÍN:
RELIEF FROM THE BALL COURT
Plate 32

There are several ball courts at Tajín. The most important one, to the south of Building V, does not take the characteristic form of a capital I since it lacks the transverse patios and the raised sidewalks which are usually found at the foot of the walls. None the less, the two large lateral walls could not have had any other purpose than to serve as part of a ball-game court. Besides, they have stone bas-reliefs at the ends and in the middle, each one consisting of four large slabs. Although all the carvings are different, many represent ball-players—that is to say, the figures are wearing thick belts which perhaps represent stone yokes with palmate stones attached to them—or they depict some ceremony connected with the same sport.

The carving on this relief shows the sacrifice of an individual dressed in the same type of clothing as the man standing behind him and holding his arms, while a third person, standing in front of him, is opening his chest with a stone sacrificial blade. The last-named wears a large headdress of plumes and seems to be speaking. Above the sacrificial victim, who is seated on a bench, is a descending deity with feet in the air, whose open legs appear immediately below the upper frieze. To the right is an individual seated on what appears to be a throne; he carries a staff in his hand. This could well be the highest-ranking person, since he is presiding over the scene without taking part in it. To the left is a fleshless figure whose head is a skull, separated from the rest of the scene by a decorative element. This probably is a god of death. The upper band, decorated with serpentine motifs, represents the sky; the lower one symbolises the earth. Here there are motifs—perhaps also of serpentine origin—which form interlaced hooks. This is the most characteristic symbol not only of Tajín itself but of the entire culture which centred around it. We find it used on countless objects, spreading as far as Teotihuacán and the Maya region. In a simpler form it is also found in Oaxaca during the Classic period.

As the four slabs which make up this relief had fallen and lain neglected for centuries, they are worn and chipped, so that they no longer fit as perfectly as they did when first erected. Also the rain has washed off the colours that were originally applied to the frieze.

PALMATE STONE *(palma)*.
TAJÍN CULTURE
Plate 33

The Tajín culture produced a great number of small carved objects, frequently of high aesthetic quality, which can be grouped into three principal types: yoke-shaped stones; *hachas*, which are thin stone heads; and palmate stones, such as the one shown in this plate. It may be assumed that the three types had a ceremonial and not a practical use, possibly associated with the ball-game players' attire. In the bas-relief from Tajín shown in the previous plate we saw individuals carrying elongated objects which project upward and which seem to emerge from the heavy bands which they wear round the waist. These objects resemble the palmate stones and like them have a concave base, which would allow them to be held in place, although with difficulty.

The palmate stones, or *palmas*, have been so called because of their resemblance to the shape of a palm leaf, but they are unlikely to have borne any symbolic relation to it. Their decoration is varied, showing animals such as crocodiles or birds (eagles and herons), or human figures, bundles of arrows or the motif of intertwined hooks so characteristic of the Tajín style. Some are entirely plain, and we know of two examples—one of which is reproduced here—which represents two human forearms in parallel position. These hands, seen from the back, have the fingers slightly separated and the finger-nails are clearly indicated.

The symbol of the hand frequently appears at sites in Mesoamerica. We find admirable representations of it in the Teotihuacán frescoes. Indeed, so important is it there, that at times the prayers do not issue from the priest's mouth but rather from his hands. Or again hands, deemed sufficiently eloquent in themselves, appear alone, without an accompanying figure. The hand played an important role in magic, and for this reason great warriors killed in battle, or women who died in child-birth, had their hands cut off. They even form part of the necklace of the terrible Aztec Coatlicue.

Palmate stones spread throughout the state of Veracruz, but some have also been found outside this region, possibly as a consequence of migrating peoples who previously lived here and later moved southward, penetrating as far as Central America. As for the dating of these objects, the whole complex of yokes, *hachas* and palmate stones is associated with the second part of the Classic period, roughly between the seventh and tenth centuries A.D.

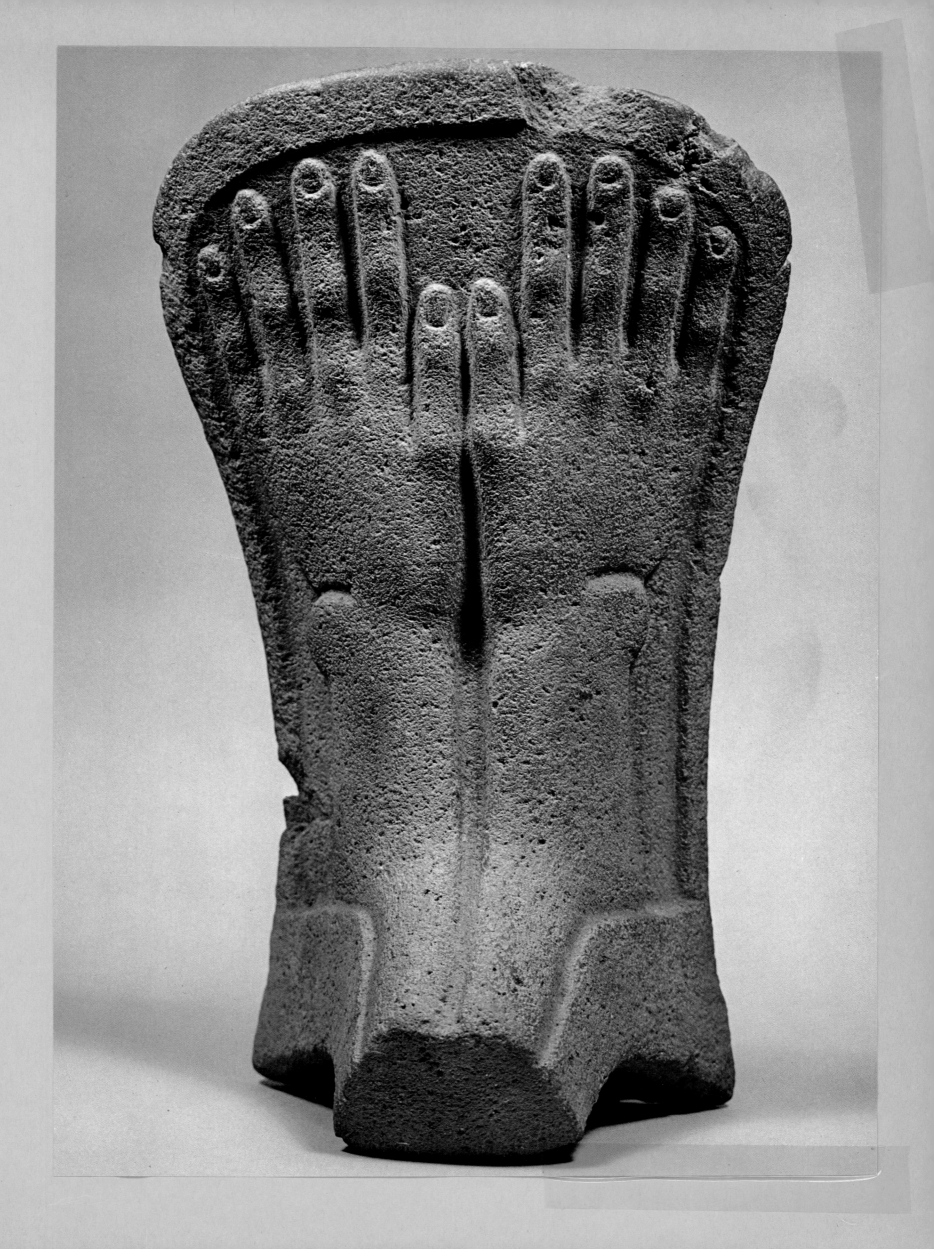

HUASTEC SCULPTURE
Plate 34

Both the figure shown here and the two figures in the next plate have a number of characteristics in common which are quite distinctive of the Huastec style. The tall conical cap, frequently associated with representations of the god Quetzalcoatl; the ear-plugs with long pendants falling over the shoulders; the general shape of the body, and the over-all treatment. Although the statues are in the round, the artist seems not yet to have discarded the idea of working on a flat surface, so that the pieces are extremely narrow when viewed in profile.

This figure wears a wide collar, or rather a pectoral upon the breast, which does not hang around the neck but seems to come out of the shoulder. He wears a kind of mini-skirt and a loin-cloth which reaches almost to the knees. This type of clothing is not often found since, according to sixteenth-century authors and on the evidence of many sculptured figures, the Huastecs went entirely nude—which must have caused a scandal among the puritanical Aztecs and Toltecs. One Toltec legend tells about a young Huastec merchant who came to sell his commodities in the market at Tula. The king's daughter saw him unclothed and fell in love with him. Ultimately the king consented to the marriage, since the princess had become paler and sadder each day on account of her love for the Huastec. But it led to a bloody revolt, for the proud Toltecs did not allow the poor nude foreigner to hold the high rank to which his marriage entitled him.

Many Huastec figures are shown with a hole in them; it is usually in the chest and probably symbolises the heart, though this statue has it in the stomach. This custom also occurs elsewhere—for example, in Teotihuacán, where the hole contained a piece of jade, a symbol of the earth which, like the heart, is precious.

TWO CARVED HUASTEC FIGURES
Plate 35

The Huastec zone—still known by this name—borders on the Gulf of Mexico in the northern part of the state of Veracruz and the southern part of the state of Tamaulipas. It also includes sections of adjoining states to the west. Within this zone are found lowlands, hot and humid, as well as a vast mountain range of considerable altitude. The Huastecs have inhabited this region since well before our era, speaking a language which is related to those of the Maya family. At some time the Huastecs either became separated from the Maya through an invasion of other peoples, or, by emigrating northwards, cut themselves off from their parent stock.

Although they live in the extreme north-east of Mesoamerica—and can therefore be regarded as only partially Mesoamericans—they have from the outset had intimate contact with other civilised peoples, as is apparent not only from objects imported into this zone, but also from Huastec influence found in Mesoamerica. For example, some Mesoamerican gods are clearly of Huastec origin, while others, typically Mesoamerican, have attributes deriving from the Huastecs. The Toltecs entered the Huastec zone, and later the Aztecs conquered all the southern part.

The region has been relatively little studied to date, but culturally the Huastecs seem to share many aspects of Mesoamerican progress, while preserving a number of features that characterise their more primitive neighbours. Among the more advanced Huastec achievements can be included its sculpture. This, it is true, did not possess the degree of complexity and refinement of some other contemporaneous sculpture, but it does show a well developed style, so distinctive that it cannot be confused with sculpture from anywhere else. This is evident in the two statues of human figures reproduced here, which are in the collection of the Museum of Anthropology in the city of Jalapa, Veracruz.

Toltecs and Mixtecs: Tula and Chichen Itzá

From the end of the ninth century until its final fall, the history of Mesoamerica can be roughly divided into two major periods; during the first the Toltec and Mixtec cultures came to the fore, whilst the second corresponded essentially to the late development of the Aztec Empire.

The name Toltec is just a general term applied to the various groups who, some time after the fall of Teotihuacán, arrived in the Central Valleys. Prior to that, connections with Mesoamerica were obscure; as members of the Nahuatl linguistic family, the Toltecs introduced the historical period. In fact, it is when their story begins in Central Mexico that we are able for the first time to identify actual people, giving names and even something of their personal history. Mixcoatl, the first chief whom we know by name, must have been an extraordinary man. His qualities and his influence reverberate all through the Indian chronicles. But even more important than Mixcoatl and still greater was to be his son, Ce Acatl Topiltzin, whom we know by the name of Quetzalcoatl. I am of course referring not to the ancient god of that name but to the historical character who was both king at Tula, the Toltec capital, and high priest of Quetzalcoatl's religion.

At the beginning of Toltec predominance in the valley, if the reconstruction of historical documents is correct, Xochicalco assumed particular importance because it is there that the son of Mixcoatl seems to have been educated. His mother came from that region and, his father having been killed, he was brought up there by his maternal grandparents. Perhaps his adherence to the religion of Quetzalcoatl dates from that time, and he later imposed the cult of this god upon the Toltecs, the worshippers of Tezcatlipoca, an evil and cruel god. In 980 Quetzalcoatl established himself in Tula to begin a short but brilliant period of 19 years, during which he not only built this great city but did it in such a manner that in time it grew to be a legend. Later chronicles describe Quetzalcoatl's reign as a sort of golden age with a beautiful Tula full of things which obviously never existed, such as walls covered with gold, emeralds, turquoise, silver or feathers. Quetzalcoatl, it was said, gave to man the corn that he had stolen in the kingdom of the dead from the old god of hell. This makes him the father of agriculture. It was also claimed that he invented the calendar, writing and books, medicine, astronomy, and the whole ceremonial ritual. Of course we know today that all these things existed before his time, but the growth of the legend shows the immense prestige he won, and it is hardly to be wondered at that later generations came to identify him with the god himself.

Tula, his capital, whose ruined monuments provide the modern archaeologist with such *Plates 36, 37* tantalising glimpses of this half-legendary place, became the model of the new Toltec style and of the new Toltec way of life. Yet, no matter how much difference we might find between it and the ancient Teotihuacán, it is quite clear that any number of features—I would say the major part of the culture—were simply inherited from that long-dead city. The Toltecs changed a few things and introduced some new ideas, but there was no real departure from the Classic style. The one basic change they seem to have made was to shift the emphasis from priestly to civil and military matters. This does not in any way mean that the warrior had not existed or played an important part in the Classic, or that the role of the priest was not to remain supremely important in the post-Classic. It is simply a question of stress, more a reorganisation of society than the building of a new one. Tangible evidence of this reorientation is provided by the representations of warriors, which, while not absent but rare in Classic art, became rather frequent in Toltec art. That these were troubled times is also indicated by the fact that many of the new cities were not laid out in open country with an imperial disdain for danger, as was Teotihuacán, but are set in hills or next to fortified sites. Whilst the old gods are for the most part preserved and actually continue to act as major deities, some gods unknown to the Classic are born, at least two of whom, Tezcatlipoca in the Toltec period and Huitzilopochtli in the late Aztec, both cruel and terrible gods, later become of major importance.

Tula, the capital. was in actual fact, much smaller than, and had little of the grandeur of, Teotihuacán. Its buildings give the impression of hasty, or rather careless construction, inspired more by the desire for a showy style than by a real love of beauty. If very few elements are really new, some are nevertheless quite interesting. Thus the Teotihuacán type of column is multiplied in Tula and vast porticos with dozens of pillars are built. The ball game becomes a major factor in the ceremonial part of the city, and to the old Classic game of the Maya, or of Monte Albán or Tajín, a new element is added—a stone ring through which the ball must pass.

It is to sculpture that the Toltecs seem to have made their major contribution. They revived with great magnificence the old Olmec idea of atlantean columns. The roof of the great temple at Tula is supported by four warriors which are not only an extraordinary aesthetic success but a typically Toltec one. Their dress, their adornments, their weapons, their attitudes—all are quite unlike those usual in the Classic period. Of course the main difference lies in the fact that they are warriors and no longer priests. Their square faces, solemn and empty, suggest the hardness of the warrior on the night of victory. Their strong bodies and short legs have the rigidity and arrogance of the soldier who combines religious fervour with his profession.

Doorways are sometimes formed by huge serpent columns but the head of the animal rests on the ground and it is the tail that forms the lintel. Carvings in low relief depict long processions of men sumptuously dressed; others show tigers walking—rather nice-looking tigers and so tame that they have a string around their neck from which hangs a bell—or terrible eagles who are eating human hearts—perhaps the blood symbolised by an already very ancient glyph. Others represent the famous man-bird-serpent that is Quetzalcoatl. Now too we first encounter the 'enclosures of serpents' and those curious reclining figures known as 'chacmools' in modern lore that are to be found in abundance, not only in the Highlands but in Yucatán.

Plate 38

In effect, most if not all of the features mentioned, together with others characteristic of Toltec culture impossible to enumerate here, appear in the great Maya–Toltec city of Chichen Itzá in the northern part of the peninsula. It is evident that Chichen Itzá rigorously copied many of the Toltec features of Tula; in some instances one would think that the same architect had built both places or that the same sculptor had done the carvings. Still, the style of Chichen Itzá is not pure Toltec but a combination of it with elements of the Maya Classic. Thus the roofs are vaulted in the Maya fashion and there are many other signs of this ancient influence. It is clear that the two cities are more or less contemporaneous, suggesting that perhaps for the first time a conqueror from the Mexican Highlands had arrived in northern Yucatán.

Plates 39–43

During this period all over Mesoamerica there are signs of advance: for example, very fine and distinctive pottery is made, and metallurgy is practised for the first time even if in a minor way. It is evident too that close ties exist between most of the areas. These suggest more clearly still than in the case of the Olmecs or of Teotihuacán, that we are dealing with an empire, a Toltec one, that extended its influence or perhaps its conquests over nearly all of Mesoamerica.

Much of what we call Toltec culture, at least in central Mexico, is really Mixtec. The Mixtecs in northern Oaxaca, who had been relatively unimportant until this time, seem to have wakened to new life. Not only did they originate a style that found favour in the rest of central Mexico, but they introduced a culture that has the distinction of being, so far as we know, the first to produce historical books. In due course Mixtec learning and Mixtec art became so popular that even during the heyday of Tenochtitlán the Aztec emperors were to bring Mixtec people to paint the hieroglyphic codices, to carve alabaster and rock crystal, to make the mosaics of turquoise and of jade, and particularly to melt gold for their wonderful jewels.   *Plates 44, 45*

We know very little of the ancient cities of the Mixteca itself but in the Valley of Oaxaca— where, as we have seen, the Mixtecs expanded in late pre-Columbian times—two important sites have been dug: Mitla and Yagul. Each shows a different architecture combining the old   *Plates 46–49* inheritance with new features. Perhaps the most striking of these is the great size of their palaces and the importance that was attached to them compared with the lesser care bestowed upon the temples of the gods.

Not all the cities and settlements of the Toltec period are new ones. At least two major places, Tajín and Xochicalco, survived the end of the Classic and continued throughout the Toltec. Tajín we have already referred to and during this last period of its life no important new developments appear to have taken place there. Xochicalco in Morelos has a long history that   *Plates 50, 51* starts in the pre-Classic and does not end until about the time of the fall of Tula. Beautifully located on top of a hill that recalls, even if it has not the grandeur of, Monte Albán, its many buildings are now mostly covered by earth and rubble; but the few laid bare so far show an interesting architecture, especially the principal pyramid whose exterior is covered with low reliefs depicting priests and gods, a great serpent, hieroglyphs, signs of fire and many other things in a style which is peculiar to Xochicalco, and seem to show a certain connection with Mayan art. This has frequently been challenged and is difficult to prove. However, there are   *Plates 52* other elements at Xochicalco which rather suggest the same thing. These include three recently discovered stelae which are inscribed all over with dates, although not in any way resembling the Long Count style. We have already mentioned Quetzalcoatl's connection with Xochicalco.

Quetzalcoatl's Tula was not all peace and prosperity. The population was a mixed one, as was that of most Mesoamerican cities. The real Toltecs, the followers of Tezcatlipoca, gradually became stronger until in 999, according to legend, Quetzalcoatl was expelled from the city. Accounts of what happened afterwards are most confusing. According to some he went first to the Gulf Coast, near what is today Coatzalcoalcos, proceeding from there to found the second great Toltec city, Chichen Itzá. But of course this may be no more than hearsay.

Following Quetzalcoatl's departure Tula lived under a long succession of kings. They it was who built the major part of the archaeological Tula that we know today. Their last king, Huemac, whose name means 'large hand', was obliged after a long reign to abandon his city and to hide in Chapultepec. According to one version, he there committed suicide. With that the Toltec dynasty at Tula ends and also the period of Toltec culture.

By the beginning of the thirteenth century the great empire seems to have collapsed entirely and only small groups survived here and there. Even so, the survivors were to matter, not only because they handed down the tradition of civilisation to the late-comers who were to appear in the Valley of Mexico a hundred years later, but because theirs was the prestige and the importance of being the descendants of Quetzalcoatl and of the legendary, fabulous Toltecs.

There follows a confusing and indeterminate epoch, usually known in the Highlands as Chichimec, on account of the name collectively given to numerous groups of lesser culture which at various times and probably from several different places of origin entered the Central Valley and became rulers, even if for very short periods.

With the fall of Toltec Chichen Itzá, a number of other cities rose to prominence in Yucatán, but they had a relatively short lease of life. Mayapán formed a league that was to disappear after a while, when the whole peninsula was divided into numerous small chiefdoms Plates 53–55 of minor importance. It is likely that Tulum, on the Caribbean Sea, came into prominence about this time, though it probably had earlier origins. We know only its ruins, nothing of its history. It is one of the first Mesoamerican cities ever seen by the Spaniards. Of very late date Plate 56 also seem to be those curious places of worship, such as the cave in Balamcanche, where offerings and ceremonies were made to the God of Rain.

TULA. ATLANTES AND SQUARE COLUMNS OF TEMPLE. Plate 36

TULA: ATLANTES AND SQUARE
COLUMNS OF TEMPLE
Plate 36

Tula, the Toltec capital, is in the region of Teotlalpan—'land of the gods'—to the north of Mexico City. Although it too is built on raised ground, it does not occupy such a spectacular position as either Monte Albán or Xochicalco. Contrary to legend, the centre of Tula is quite small, being built mainly around two plazas. Separating the two is a large palace whose roofs were supported by a multitude of columns ranged along the whole northern side of the plaza. Forty-two of these columns formed an immense portico which led to the most spectacular building at Tula: the Temple of Tlahuizcalpantecuhtli.

This 'brief' Nahuatl name refers to the god of the planet Venus, the morning and evening star which is associated with the figure of the great god Quetzalcoatl. We should recall that not the god but the man who bore his name was the founder of this city and the initiator of the Toltec state.

Upon the pyramid which served as a base stood the great temple; of this nothing remains today except enormous columns which supported the roof. This plate shows two of the rectangular pilasters bearing numerous incised motifs; and, in front of these, two of the four warriors upon whose heads the lintel rested. They are composed of four sections which fit together perfectly. The top section comprises the head with its great crown decorated with jade beads and eagle feathers. Below this is a smaller block forming the upper part of the body which carries an enormous breast-plate in the form of a butterfly on the chest. A knotted belt to which is attached a large disk worn on the warrior's back characterises the next section down. The short sturdy legs of the bottom section wear ankle bracelets and bands, and their sandals have a serpent motif carved on the sides. The arms are represented in flat form at the flanks of the body; in the right hand they carry an *atlatl*, or spear-thrower, and in the left a bundle of darts. The total height of these figures is 11·80 metres.

TULA: COATEPANTLI
Plate 37

To the north of the Temple of Venus and a short distance from its base, the Toltecs built a wall enclosing a small space which must have been used for special ceremonies. This wall became known as Coatepantli, 'wall of serpents', and the idea which originated in Tula was repeated later in Chichimec and Aztec structures. It is found, although in quite different form, around the pyramid of Tenayuca, and the group of buildings which formed the Main Temple of Tenochtitlán was surrounded by a wall decorated with serpents. In this photograph we see part of the Coatepantli in Tula. Upon a sloping foundation 90 centimetres high, rests the equivalent of the classic panel of the structures of Central Mexico. Here it takes the form of three horizontal bands. The upper and lower bands contain only frets, very imperfect in comparison with the precise ones at Mitla. The central band shows the god Tlahuiz-calpantecuhtli, whose temple we have seen in the previous plate. In this case the god is in difficulties: a serpent is devouring him and the only parts which still show are the head—which is a skull—and an arm to the bones of which some flesh still adheres. Curiously, one of the god's legs—partly divested of flesh—has escaped and still wears a sandal. Some merely decorative merlons which represent the transverse section of a conch shell—another symbol of Quetzalcoatl—give the finishing touch to this wall which, without the merlons, measures 2·20 metres in height.

XLAPAK: CORNER OF PALACE
Plate 38

If we know little enough about the Puuc cities, we know still less about sites such as Xlapak even though it is very near Labná. Its buildings have not yet been explored, and only part of them are visible in the jungle; as, for instance, this beautiful corner of a palace in purest Puuc style with its three superposed masks of the God of Rain. A cornice with drums of short columns separate the decorated area above from the plain surface below. In the centre the masks assume a geometric form, while to their left can be seen the beginning of a *xicolcoliuhqui*, the fret which in a multitude of variations represents a stylised serpent, and from the end of the Preclassic was used in all Nuclear Mesoamerica.

This photograph evokes the romantic atmosphere of drawings from the middle of the nineteenth century in which wild plants are shown growing in profusion over stones carved with so much effort and application in ancient times, slowly destroying the masonry until finally it falls to the ground.

John Lloyd Stephens, well named the Herodotus of Mayan archaeology, illustrates his second book, *Incidents of Travel in Yucatán*, which appeared in 1843, with numerous drawings made by that enterprising London architect, Frederick Catherwood, who accompanied him on his trips. Current tastes, the silent solitude of the ruins, and his profound interest in the ancient Maya and their works, led Catherwood to populate his very accurate drawings with trees and plants, which far from weakening their archaeological value, renders them more realistic.

CHICHEN ITZÁ: 'CHURCH'
Plate 39

The great city of Chichen Itzá shows at least two clearly-distinguishable periods in its monuments. One corresponds to the second part of the Classic period in the Mayan world, from A.D. 650 to 900; and the other dates from after the time when the Toltecs took over. Although various buildings of the former period were altered and re-used in later times, the majority remained unchanged and form the group of ruins known as Chichen Viejo (Old Chichen). The general style of this older part resembles the Puuc style of Uxmal and near-by cities in many particulars, but it also shows rather conspicuous differences. Thus, as Eric Thompson has pointed out, Puuc elements such as triple entrances, columns imbedded in the wall, models of huts in stone, decoration of the medial cornice, and serpents shown in profile are unknown or very rare in the Chichen Itzá of that period.

One of the buildings of Chichen Viejo built in the older style is that known as 'the Church'. It is a rather small, rectangular structure, having only one entrance in front, as shown in the photograph. The lower section of the façade is plain and all the decoration is concentrated on the upper part and on the comb, which is a continuation upwards of the façade, just as in the Mirador at Labná (Plate 26). This gives the impression that the building is much taller than it really is. The frieze and the comb are decorated with elaborate masks in the centre and at the corners. On either side of the central mask of the frieze are four pairs of panels. Each contains an animal—an armadillo, a snail, a tortoise, and a crab—which represent the four *bacabs*, deities who support the heavens, one in each corner.

CHICHEN ITZÁ:
SERPENT COLUMNS OF TEMPLE
OF THE JAGUARS
Plate 40

The ball court at Chichen Itzá is not only the largest yet discovered but it possesses a number of features which make it rank among the most interesting structures of ancient Mexico. Like all ball courts in Mesoamerica, it has the shape of a capital I, flanked on both long sides by platforms with stairways facing outward. Upon its own foundation set into the eastern platform rises the Temple of the Jaguars, whose main façade faces the ball court. The interior of the temple takes the form of two large vaulted halls in parallel. The façade, of which this plate shows a detail, has an entrance portico with two massive columns in the shape of serpents. The heads of the reptiles rest on the floor, their bodies form the columns themselves, and their tails—with rattles and plumes—support the architrave. From its elements we know that this is a plumed rattlesnake, which is the symbol of Quetzalcoatl. The upper part of the façade, unlike the purely Mayan buildings, has a frieze adorned with shields alternating with walking tigers, so similar to those of Tula—the Toltec capital of the central Highlands—that they might be the work of the same artist.

Thus this interesting building combines features of traditional Mayan architecture, such as the corbelled arch and the general lines of the façade, with typically Toltec elements such as columns formed of serpents head-down, shields, and friezes of strolling tigers.

The temple undoubtedly dates from the zenith of Chichen Itzá in the Maya–Toltec period, which begins towards the end of the tenth century A.D.

Those who wonder why a temple should be intimately associated with a site used for sports such as the ball game should bear in mind that in Mesoamerica this game has profound religious connotations, being regarded as a ceremony in which the players take part in a ritual act. The loser used to be ritually decapitated—or so legend has it. From his severed neck—as seen in the bas-reliefs of the courts at Tajín and Chichen Itzá—instead of blood, seven serpents spurt out. Occasionally plants with flowers are substituted for some of these.

CHICHEN ITZÁ:
TEMPLE OF THE JAGUARS AND
TEMPLE OF THE EAGLES
Plate 41

This plate shows the exterior façade of the Temple of the Jaguars, seen from across Toltec Chichen Itzá—where the Castillo, the Temple of the Warriors, and the ball court are located. Indeed, the narrow stairway on the left leads to the farther side of the upper building (shown in the preceding plate), from where the ball game can be observed. On the side we see here there is a projecting room on the level of the plaza; it too has a vaulted roof. The entrance, in the form of a portico, is divided into three parts by pillars decorated with reliefs of the God of Rain. In front is a throne in the form of a jaguar.

The interior is entirely decorated with painted bas-reliefs, splendidly executed and of great interest. They are in four rows and depict persons variously attired. In the top row the figures approach an individual seated on a tiger throne, surrounded by the sun's rays; in the row immediately below, the figures are moving towards another individual standing in the coils of a ferocious serpent. This is reminiscent of a very old motif already seen in a bas-relief of La Venta—that is, more than 1,500 years earlier. The two lower rows have numerous figures with great feathered head-dresses and diverse objects in their hands. The decoration as a whole combines elements that characterise both groups then inhabiting Chichen Itzá; thus some of the people are dressed like Toltecs, while other details are typical of Mayan art.

The small structure on the right is known as the Temple of the Eagles. It is not really a temple but a low platform for performing ceremonies in the open air. On all four sides is a staircase, as is customary with this type of adoratory. Serpents' bodies ascend the low balustrade in a style characteristic of Chichen, to end in rounded heads. The building derives its name from the plaques in low relief on the side panels, showing eagles and jaguars devouring hearts. They are identical with those which appear on the Temple of Venus at Tula.

CHICHEN ITZÁ: CASTILLO
Plate 42

The Castillo, located more or less in the centre of Chichen Itzá, is the city's principal structure dating from the Toltec period. The name Castillo (Castle) is really a misnomer for in fact it is a rather small temple placed on top of a large pyramid, a combination characteristic of Central Mexico. Nevertheless, both the outside of the pyramid and the inside of the temple differ in certain important particulars from other structures in this and the southern Maya area. The quadrangular pyramid, with its nine diminishing sections and angles rounded off, rises to a height of 24 metres without the temple which is 6 metres high.

Four enormous stairways with 91 steps each—making a total of 364—lead up to the temple. The numbers are all ritualistic: the nine is related to the gods of death, and the 364 is evidently the closest the Toltecs could get to the days of the year. With the step that circles the temple, however, the total comes to 365. The low balustrades of the main staircase terminate in large serpent-heads.

The temple itself has a curious plan. Three of the stairways lead to doors opening onto an interior passage that does not connect with the vestibule and sanctuary; the main stairway alone gives access to these. The vestibule entrance is divided into three by two columns representing serpents head-down, as in the Temple of the Jaguars. On top of the roof, instead of the roof comb that crowns Classic Maya temples, merlons shaped like a sectioned snail shell ran all around the edges. In short, all the Maya and Toltec elements of the building are blended to form a new and sumptuous architecture.

The building we see conceals a very similar one inside. When the pyramid was enlarged the older structure was, fortunately, left intact. Excavation work— which had to be by tunnelling—showed the interior sanctuary to be still furnished as in its prime. Near the doorway lay a chacmool, or effigy of a reclining god, and at the back stood a throne in the shape of a wonderful jaguar, still painted brilliant red and with spots represented by jade disks.

CHICHEN ITZÁ:
CARACOL, CASTILLO
AND TEMPLE OF THE WARRIORS,
FROM THE NUNNERY
Plate 43

This view of Chichen, taken from the walls of the Nunnery—a name no more justified here than at Uxmal—shows the Caracol with the Castillo and the Temple of the Warriors.

The disposition alone of these buildings—among the most important of Toltec Chichen Itzá—is quite different from that of cities in Central Mexico, which followed a much more elaborate plan carried to its culmination at Teotihuacán. At Chichen, despite the influence of the Toltecs who were direct heirs of Teotihuacán, there is not such regularity, the temples being placed if not at random, at least more freely and without taking others into account.

The Caracol, some 450 metres south-east of the Castillo, owes its name to an interior spiral staircase popularly called 'snail-shell stairway'. The building actually represents a series of different periods, since it was altered and changed at various times, both where the central structure and the platforms surrounding it are concerned. The circular tower is built upon square foundations, giving the building a curious aspect which led Eric Thompson to quip that the Caracol was built to demonstrate the saying: 'You can't fit a round peg in a square hole.' Although not very pleasing aesthetically, this round tower is unique, with its stairway in the centre and two concentric walls enclosing high vaulted rooms. The stairway is barely wide enough for one person. The Caracol is said to have been an astronomical observatory but there is little indication of this since the upper part is badly conserved. Its total height including the platform is now 41·5 metres, although it was originally a little more.

MIXTEC PAINTED VASES
Plate 44

During the tenth century a very important culture emerged in northern Oaxaca and the Valley of Puebla which we call Mixteca-Puebla. In general it was not interested in great sculpture or sensational monuments but concentrated its talents on finely worked small objects with an exquisite finish. It is here that the most beautiful codices of ancient Mexico, relating the history of kings, were written; here the most delicate objects were carved of bone, alabaster and precious stones; metallurgy reached its greatest splendour, and potters produced the most perfect polychrome vessels of which we know. This is exemplified by these two vases decorated with themes related to death and sacrifice, both of which were basic to the indigenous religion and permeate even activities that seem quite remote from them.

In this case little colour was used, perhaps to harmonise with the chosen theme; others manifest an enormous range—not only the usual colours of Mesoamerican ceramics but others which are rare, such as pale blue, pink, grey, and silver. Motifs and combinations are extremely varied although most of them have a religious symbolism. Some vessels resemble the page of a codex; they are drawn in a like style, use similar colours, and represent the same gods or objects. The success of this Mixtec culture was such that in their days of glory the Aztecs—successors in time—brought to their capital Mixtec potters, gold- and silversmiths, and lapidaries, since only these artists could make objects worthy of display in the new imperial capital, Tenochtitlán.

MIXTEC GOLD ORNAMENTS
FROM MONTE ALBÁN
Plate 45

While Mixtec ceramics are remarkable, their metalwork is even more so. The use of gold, silver and copper began only very late in Mesoamerica, the oldest metal objects we know dating no further back than to the tenth century A.D. It is almost certain that knowledge of working metals came from South America—where it was known much earlier—and diffused northward through Central America. Although in some regions tools were made, for example copper axes, metallurgy in Mesoamerica in general was applied rather to personal ornaments. Jewellery, mostly in gold, was a prominent feature. Besides the simpler procedures using sheets of metal or filigree work, the Mixtec smiths handled to perfection the much more complex *cire-perdue* process of casting, the only method by which very fine jewellery such as that shown on this plate can be produced. All these articles were found at Monte Albán in the famous Tomb 7 where some Mixtec chiefs—surely men of great importance—were buried. In its last period, which we call Monte Albán V, this was not a Zapotec city; it was occupied by Mixtecs.

The little mask represents the god Xipe, 'Our Lord the Flayed One', with the skin of the sacrificial victim's thigh placed over the god's face. His hair, longer on one side than on the other, indicates that he is a warrior. The large pectoral, with the face of the god of death, has two dates on the plaques below; one shows the year Ten Wind and the other the year Eleven House. This probably indicates a correction of the calendar. The top four portions of the pendant in the centre show a ball court in the usual shape, a solar disk, and two rectangular plaques depicting a stone sacrificial blade and a toad, symbolising the moon and the earth respectively. A descending eagle from whose beak hangs a butterfly can be seen on another of the pieces.

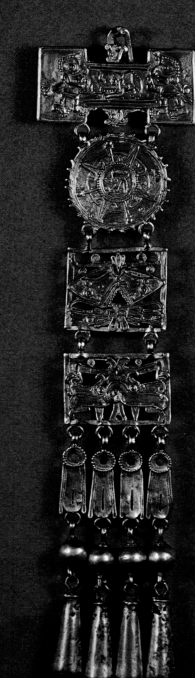

MITLA: THE PALACE
Plate 46

In the last centuries before the Spanish conquest the Mixtecs, as we have seen, occupied part of the Valley of Oaxaca. In the eastern end of it they constructed buildings in a style and with basic concepts very different from those prevailing at Monte Albán. It is not for its religious monuments that the best known of these cities—Mitla—is outstanding, but for various palaces that in their architecture recall the exquisite detail which the Mixtecs worked into smaller objects. To a rough core of rocks and mud the builders of Mitla applied remarkable facings. The large stones used for this purpose are carved with great perfection while the panels are formed of a stone mosaic. Each stone had to be specially cut to fit a particular space and then was set in with the greatest precision not only to build up the composite design but to make it a firm construction, since no mortar was used between the pieces. Motifs are varied but in almost every case stylisations of serpents appear; some of these would now be impossible to decipher were it not for the Mitla frets which show the successive steps leading from a realistic rendering of an animal to its geometric stylisation. It has been calculated that for the mosaics in the various palaces of Mitla more than 130,000 separate pieces were used. As each one had to be carved separately, the time and effort involved indicates that an abundance of labour was diverted from work in the fields or other essential occupations, a sign that the nobility possessed both power and prestige.

MITLA:
THE PALACE AND CHRISTIAN
CHURCH
Plate 47

One of the palaces at Mitla, known nowadays as the 'Palace of the Church', was formed of three large patios surrounded by rooms, built and decorated in the manner of other similar structures. Over a lintel in one of the patios are still visible traces of an interesting mural fresco painted in a style identical to that of the Mixtec codices. In the sixteenth century a church of considerable size was built over part of the Prehispanic structure, naturally destroying much of it; indeed, it is still possible to identify worked stones from the old palace, which were re-used for building the church.

This view shows the partially conserved exterior corner of the Prehispanic palace, backed by a row of what are popularly called organ cactuses, often used in this region to mark the boundaries of property and even to align the streets of native villages. Beyond rise the walls and cupolas of the church, interesting not so much in itself—it is not one of the most beautiful—but because it completes the various facets of Mexico: the Prehispanic, the modern indigenous and the European. The barren mountains in the background encircle this eastern end of the Valley of Oaxaca, which is the most arid of the entire region.

YAGUL: GENERAL VIEW
Plate 48

Very similar to Mitla in many respects is near-by Yagul, likewise in the Valley of Oaxaca. The part of this ancient city so far explored consists of an immense platform with raised areas at various levels. On the highest of these is the 'Palace of Six Patios', a huge structure with over thirty rooms, most of which are ranged around these patios. The whole unit has only one entrance that leads into a long hallway, dividing it into two unequal parts. In the western section there are four, in the eastern two, patios—these latter better constructed and more elaborate. Here too, as at Mitla, portions of the exterior walls were covered by a stone mosaic, but this has disappeared and explorations have recovered but few of its remains, possibly owing to stone from the ancient city having been used to build a great part of the modern town of Tlacolula, its neighbour. On a lower level is another large unit comprising the *Sala del Consejo* (Assembly Hall)—a vast room similar to that at the entrance to the main palace at Mitla but without the monolithic columns—other civic buildings, and the ball court. There are further, bigger patios surrounded by large rooms. Only a tall pyramid, now in very bad condition, suggests that a temple once stood here. Much higher up, from where this photograph was taken, is the fortress, formed in part of natural rocks and in part by stone walls.

At Yagul, in contrast with Monte Albán but like at Mitla, more importance was attached to the civil and military aspects, and less to the religious side. The city's position high above the fertile valley—perhaps for defence—provides a panorama of exceptional beauty.

THE BALL COURT AT
XOCHICALCO
Plate 49

On the uppermost level of the ancient city of Xochicalco, built on a moderately high hill, are the remains of a fortress. This would indicate that the site could be defended, unlike Teotihuacán which is situated in a broad plain.

On a flat area and on a lower level than the monument to Quetzalcoatl is situated the enormous ball court seen in this plate. It is 69 metres long, being therefore much larger than the one at Monte Albán but almost identical to the one at Tula, not only in size but in general design. Both are laid out in the customary fashion, the field being in the shape of a capital I flanked on each side by a sloping embankment ending in a wall; in the centre of each of the two walls is a large stone ring, one of which can be clearly seen in this view. It is assumed that the ball was meant to pass through these rings, an event which must have been rare indeed if we take into consideration the manner of playing, the size of the ball and the relatively small orifice. The platforms behind the walls, where the remains of small buildings can still be seen, are not identical: on the north side (to the right in this photo) the natural rock has been utilised, to the south the platform begins on a lower level and follows the slant of the hill. Slopes or batters, porticos and staircases compensate for this difference.

In middle distance can be seen remains of a building known as Malinche, joined to the ball court by a broad avenue 50 metres long.

Xochicalco was one of the first sites to which Mexican archaeologists of the eighteenth century devoted their attention. Alexander von Humboldt, who never visited Xochicalco, availed himself of these pioneer works in order to write a far from accurate description of the site. We now know not only a great deal more about the building described by Humboldt and other scholars of his day, but of various additional ones that have since been explored and in which a great number of objects were found.

The pyramid that was initially uncovered is still, however, outstanding among the monuments at Xochicalco. It is not for its size that it is remarkable—since it is relatively small—but for the low reliefs that originally covered the entire structure. The reliefs on the lower section comprising a tall sloping base and a wide cornice corresponding to the panel in Teotihuacán-style architecture, show an abundance of motifs. The detail to be seen in this plate represents a plumed serpent—the god Quetzalcoatl—with a skilfully carved head from which a forked tongue protrudes, an undulating body, and a tail terminating in feathers. As with all great ceremonial serpents of Mesoamerica, the serpent is depicted with an eyebrow, as well as a beard under the lower jaw.

One of the spaces formed by the reptile's curves contains hieroglyphs with the sign for fire. The other is even more important, in that it shows a seated figure holding one hand over the breast and wearing an enormous headdress of plumes. The posture, the design and the general aspect of this individual recall—even if it is only remotely—a Maya priest.

ALABASTER VESSEL FROM
XOCHICALCO
Plate 51

Of all the sites in Central Mexico, Xochicalco shows most influence from other areas. Excavations here have recovered stelae with Zapotec and Pacific coast elements; there are echoes of Teotihuacán, and later, also clearly Toltec contributions. Xochicalco has a long history which extends from the Pre-classic until the twelfth century A.D.; it seems to have been a centre where peoples and cultures from many areas converged. Nevertheless, it would be wrong to assume that Xochicalco did not produce a style of its own. There were periods when it created a very precise, refined art, as certain characteristic tablets, sculptures, pottery and a number of other objects show. One example is the recently discovered alabaster vessel—here published in colour for the first time. It bears a rectangle painted in pastel-like tones. Above a hieroglyph appears a bird with its head facing downwards, wings half open, and the four plumes of its tail forming the upper part of the composition. This could be a 'Cuauhtemoc', the descending eagle that is a symbol of the setting sun, a motif found in many different parts of Mesoamerica and later adopted by the last Aztec emperor. We have already seen it on a gold Mixtec pectoral which came from Tomb 7 of Monte Albán (Plate 45). Aztec statuary was later to use the same motif magnificently carved.

TENAYUCA: PYRAMID
Plate 52

The great temple of Tenayuca on the outskirts of Mexico City is among the few known buildings dating from the period subsequent to the fall of Tula but prior to the triumph of Tenochtitlán. In this period (1200–1400), deceptively called Chichimec, its builders certainly copied the old architecture inherited from Tula, as the Aztecs were to do later. A characteristic feature is the *coatepantli*, or wall of serpents; here, however, instead of running all round the pyramid, this chain of rather realistic reptiles encompasses three sides only. Also it does not really form a wall setting off an area devoted to occult ceremonies, as at Tula.

The principal innovation at Tenayuca makes for economy: instead of the pyramid serving as a base to support a single temple, as had previously been the rule, it now holds two, each with its own stairway and low balustrade. This idea was to be used again in the great temple of Tenochtitlán where the Aztecs placed over a single gigantic base both a temple to the God of War and a temple to the God of Rain.

We cannot judge the nature of the city or town that surrounded Tenayuca since the area is now entirely built up, making archaeological exploration difficult. Since the temple itself was in ruins, the work of reconstruction was considerable, but it has been very carefully done. Of course, like all temples in Mesoamerica, it was originally covered with stucco and painted in vivid colours.

TULUM: FROM THE SOUTH
Plate 53

On the east coast of the Yucatán Peninsula, facing the island of Cozumel, stand the ruins of Tulum. The coast is generally flat, but the builders of this city chose a promontory overlooking the sea. That they were thinking in terms of defence is indicated not only by the situation but by the wall with which they surrounded Tulum. It is one of the extremely rare cities in Mesoamerica that were truly walled in; the great majority were either open or protected by a partly natural fortress not designed to impede access to its centre. Yagul and Xochicalco are cases in point. There the fortress served only as refuge for the population while an invader was taking the city; once the temple was burned the conqueror withdrew.

One of the pioneering expeditions made before Cortes came on the scene was that of Juan de Grijalva. In an account of the undertaking, the chaplain of his fleet tells how the party left the Island of Cozumel on 7 May, 1518, and steered towards the coast. 'We saw three large towns which were almost two miles distant one from the other, and in them were many stone houses, very big towers and many thatched houses. We should have liked to enter these places if the captain had allowed it; but having been refused permission for this, we sailed day and night along the coast, and the next day a little before sunset we perceived far in the distance a town or village so big that the city of Seville could not appear larger or better; and a huge tower was seen in it.'

It is almost certain that this town as large as Seville was Tulum, at that time still inhabited and prosperous. The tower which the Spaniards saw must have been the building known today as the Castillo, which dominates the city on top of the cliffs.

TULUM: FROM THE NORTH
Plate 54

Its great historical interest apart, Tulum is one of the most beautiful sites occupied by any city of ancient Mexico. Its layout is similar to that of numerous other sites in eastern Yucatán, but with certain peculiarities of its own. Chapels or very small temples abound, the roofs, unlike the vaulted stone roofs of the Maya, are rather flat and of wood, the lintels of doorways—slightly embedded in the wall—are formed of sunken panels, and side-walks circle the buildings. These small differences are of course not peculiar to this region but such features seem to be more frequently encountered here than in any other area.

That Tulum is a late city of Yucatán is evident not only from the report mentioned in the previous note, but also from its archaeology. On the buildings some elements of sculpture, painting and decoration indicate Toltec influence, although not all the features of this culture we have encountered at Chichen Itzá are present here. It is very probable that the history of the Tulum we know began in the eleventh century A.D.

TULUM: CASTILLO AND TEMPLE
OF THE FRESCOES
Plate 55

The walls of Tulum enclose a rectangular space measuring 380 metres from north to south and 165 from east to west. Within this area the remains of some 50 buildings of various sizes have been found. The most central ones—shown in this plate—are distributed around a plaza; others form a kind of street, and still others do not show any precise planning. In this view we are facing east towards the front of the Castillo, beyond which is the sea. The Castillo is the tallest and largest building of Tulum, and the topmost point of the promontory was chosen for its location. It still betrays several distinct building periods. The north and south ends are the oldest. The central part of the old building was filled in later to serve as a base on which was erected a temple, composed of the sanctuary and a portico, steps being added to the stairway in order to reach this new level. The portico—divided into three entrances by serpentine columns similar to those at Chichen, although much inferior—can be clearly seen in the photograph. As frequently occurs at Tulum, the exterior walls slant slightly outwards from the bottom up, while the door-jambs by contrast, slant inwards. Over each of the entrances is a niche with stucco figures. The central one—the best preserved—represents a descending god, such as is also found in other temples at Tulum. These descending gods are a recurrent feature in the art and religion of Mesoamerica. The Aztecs called them Tzontemoc and they symbolised the sun as it goes down in the late afternoon. But at Tulum they may have had a different connotation; they could represent rain, lightning, or perhaps even the bee—all of which have on occasion been portrayed in some such manner. The rooms on either side of the stairway were the last additions made to the building.

The building in the right foreground is known as the Temple of the Frescoes, and here too various periods of construction can be discerned. The oldest part now forms the ground floor to which access is gained through a portico with four columns. On top of this is a newer temple with horizontal sections separated by mouldings above a base with characteristic batter. A large part of the façade was decorated with embossed motifs made of stucco, of which some traces remain, as well as with paintings carried out in an interesting manner combining themes and forms to be found in both Maya and Aztec pictorial manuscripts. It is from these paintings that the building derived its name.

RITUAL CAVE AT
BALAMCANCHE
Plate 56

While the temples of Palenque, Uxmal, Chichen Itzá and many other cities represent the great urban architecture of the Maya, as well as the official religion and ceremonial worship of their culture, quite often places have come to light which reveal popular cults and magic practised not by priests and chiefs, but by the common people. One such, discovered only a few years ago, does not involve a man-made building but is a cave used by people of the town for their rites—perhaps marginal to the orthodox religion.

The natural stage provided by this cave near Chichen Itzá—full of stalagmites and here and there still containing small pools of water—was used by the Maya as a sanctuary for invoking aid from the God of Rain. Hence the numerous braziers with the face of this god crudely depicted on them. Charcoal and incense were burned in these to produce smoke for magic ceremonies; they are painted red and blue. There are also stone braziers with figures in a style recalling Toltec work, spindle whorls, small millstones used to grind seeds—principally corn—and convert it into dough, as well as vessels in various shapes. The style of all these pieces indicates that the cave was used for worship in the last centuries before the conquest, and very probably also in an earlier period when the great Maya culture of Yucatán had already become decadent. No buildings were constructed at this time and it is probable that the priestly caste which had led the Maya culture to such great heights was in full decline.

The Aztec Empire: Tenochtitlán

Around this time the Aztecs begin to assume importance. They had already appeared in Central Mexico much earlier and are likely to have been there by the time of the fall of Tula. Their beginnings are inauspicious. As a very small and unimportant tribe led by four chief priests whose only valuable possession was a strange package that contained a statue of the god Huitzilo-pochtli, till then unknown, they wander from place to place. After 1215 they arrive in the Valley, where they continue their rather nomadic type of life. They are badly received wherever they go and soon sent packing, since those around them regard their conduct as insupportable. Their reputation for being cruel, false to their word, and women-stealers was well-merited; extremely brave in the field and scornful of death, they have to rely on fighting for their very existence. They finally succeed in remaining for a number of years in Chapultepec until battle is joined; they are vanquished and taken prisoners, their chief is sacrificed in Culhuacán, and the others become practically slaves of the Culhuas. These Culhuas, descendants of the Toltecs, retained the pride, if not the power, of their ancestors. They sent these Aztecs, the true fore-runners of the Mexicans, to a region where life was virtually impossible, since little more than serpents were found there. Nevertheless, the Mexicans managed to survive, but only by per-petrating a number of horrible acts which made them so hated that they were again expelled and had nowhere to go. It was then that they took refuge in the last available place, a little marshy island in the Lake of Texcoco. This unpromising site was to become Tenochtitlán, their capital, and in the course of time the centre of a great empire.

The Aztecs lived on their island very modestly at first, slowly improving their lot, until in 1428 they won a major battle against the principal power in the valleys and a few years later the war as a whole. In this way Tenochtitlán came to control the various groups in the Valley of Mexico, and the imperialistic expansion under Izcoatl, the fourth emperor, began. His heir, Moctezuma I, not only immensely extended the empire but set about building a capital worthy of it, no longer in mud and reeds but in stone. Under him most of the major monuments and even some of the huge carvings that were to lend Aztec art imperishable fame were embarked on. The city continued to grow, just as did the empire, under a succession of emperors until the time of Moctezuma II and the arrival of Cortes.

By then it was not only at the head of the Mesoamerican world politically, economically and religiously, but had through conquest and tribute, managed to establish itself on a sound economic basis. It had acquired architects, sculptors and all manner of craftsmen who were busy building temples for the gods and palaces for the nobility. The amount of sculpture of all types *Plates 57–59* and sizes recovered from the ruins of Tenochtitlán is astonishing. Some of the objects must be counted among the greatest expressions of Indian art and thinking. Others are used for the first time as a vehicle for certain ideas, for example the Stone of Tizoc, which relates this emperor's *Plate 60* actual conquests. The idea it conveys is that of empire, even though the emperor is dressed in the garb of a god.

A proud aristocracy soon took control. It was formed of the high priests, army chiefs, leading statesmen, the imperial family, and even a few of the more important merchants. These had a status and led a life far removed from the tribal existence of the poor man. We know this élite much better of course than we know the earlier aristocracies of the Toltecs or the Teotihuacanos, but everything suggests that it had modelled itself on the latter, and that its ideas and methods were a legacy from these, their antecedents. Its power lay in its command, prestige, culture and inherited position. To these must be added the confidence and support of the gods, and having the great god Huitzilopochtli himself speak to them and tell them how to act. Gradually, this direct link with the god diminished, and in time virtually disappeared. With the expansion of the group it became impracticable, but the prestige remained.

The emperor was lord over everybody and everything; his authority was absolute. He was head priest of Huitzilopochtli, as well as great military chief. Though his position was not hereditary but elective, the election was always confined to the members of one family, just as in the Holy Roman Empire. In his person, at least in the time of Moctezuma II, were combined not only all the wealth, luxury and pleasure that his society could provide, but almost the rank of a god. Court ceremonies rivalled Asiatic ones in splendour and despotism. Nobody could gainsay him. That is why he took the name of Lord of the Toltecs—he was basking in the reflected glory of his ancestors whose renown he had inherited. Moctezuma II was a good soldier, and a very zealous priest; sometimes, too—and here he broke with tradition—he was a thinker. Perhaps it was the very urbanity of this man, full of humour and distinction, his refinement, his generosity and his fatalism that engendered the irresolution and weakness that he showed before Cortes. His more remarkable qualities were fatal to his person, and to his empire.

The Aztec cultural achievement has been called a miracle, in the same way as historians used to speak of the Greek miracle. And just as in the case of the Greeks, the more we have come to learn of their antecedents the more light it has shed on how this miracle came to pass. The Aztecs could certainly not, in the course of no more than a century, have built up from scratch such a complex urban society, such great art, and such an evolved pantheon. That they derived their cultural inheritance from the peoples who preceded them in the more advanced regions of Mesoamerica will have become evident even from this brief survey of Mexican archaeology and ancient history. To these peoples they owed their economic system, their social and political organisation, their religion and their artistic and intellectual patrimony. We are able to trace the line of this inheritance more clearly now, at least from the great days of Teotihuacán, when so many of the new developments took place, onwards. Although the Aztecs knew next to nothing of Teotihuacán, they felt in a confused sort of way how much they owed to the Toltecs, their ancestors upon whom the mantle of Teotihuacán culture had fallen. Their urge to claim Toltec ancestry—no matter how speculative it might have been in the strictly genealogical sense—is to be seen in all Aztec culture and political thinking. This accounts for the Aztec emperor's setting so much store by having as consort a princess from the Culhuacán house, since the Culhuas were supposed to be the direct heirs of Tula. In 1428, moreover, after the great victory that gave the Aztecs dominance over the Valley people, the new title their leader chose was not as might be expected 'Lord of the Aztecs', but 'Lord of the Culhuas'— which is tantamount to calling himself lord of the Toltecs. Thereby he wished to signify that his people had not only become the leading political and military power, but taken over all the honour and prestige of the Toltecs, filling the void caused by the fall of Tula.

MALINALCO. TEMPLE CARVED OUT OF CLIFF-SIDE. Plate 57

MALINALCO: TEMPLE CARVED
OUT OF CLIFF-SIDE
Plate 57

Malinalco is an extraordinary site, in that it comprises a main temple and some minor buildings for the most part carved out of the flank of a steep cliff. Almost no actual building was done at this site, the rock being hollowed out to give form to the interior circular structure with thatched roof seen in this plate, as well as to stairways with low balustrades, walls and even to pieces of sculpture. The interior, consisting of a low-ceilinged circular room with a low bench round the sides is remarkable—although unfortunately not photogenic. Above the low bench and in the middle of the room are sculptured figures, also carved from the rock itself, which represent instead of eagles and a jaguar, the stretched skins of these animals. The doorway, unfortunately now incomplete, was perhaps an arch, which would be unique in Mesoamerican art.

Malinalco was conquered by the Aztecs in 1476. A few years later, in 1501, the Emperor Ahuitzotl initiated the carving of the living rock. Under his successor Moctezuma II work continued until 1515, when it was interrupted before all the parts had been finished. By this time, however, the principal building was already in use, the temple being devoted to secret meetings of the great Aztec military orders of the Eagle and the Jaguar Knights. These orders of knighthood, which were not only military but had strong religious and magic connotations as well, perhaps gave rise to the belief that Malinalco was a place where witchcraft was practised. Even today in the small city at the foot of the hill witches abound—in the shape of medicine men and those who cast the evil eye on people—whose presence and practices at one and the same time so attract and frighten the indigenous population.

AZTEC STONE SCULPTURE
OF COATLICUE
Plate 58

When in 1790 exploration was begun in the Central Plaza of Mexico City, some extremely important Aztec sculptures were discovered. Among these was a colossal statue, 2.56 metres high, representing the goddess Coatlicue—'she of the skirt made of serpents'. The viceroy Revillagigedo ordered that these statues be conserved 'as precious monuments which reveal the high culture that enlightened the Indian nation in times before its conquest . . .', an attitude quite different from the earlier one which for religious and political reasons demanded the destruction of all ancient remains. The statue of Coatlicue was moved to the University and ultimately transferred to the National Museum in 1866. Justino Fernandez has described this sculpture as follows: '(It) has the shape of a great cross with a robust trunk, short arms, and well-proportioned head; it is not surprising therefore that the diverse elements are arranged in perfect symmetry about a vertical axis. The body is divided into four zones of practically equal proportions. These are well demarcated by horizontal lines at different levels, corresponding to the legs, serpent skirt, thorax and bicephalic mass; and from the trunk project the folded arms, which by virtue of the elements composing them again divide the height of the trunk into two parts.' The statue is full of symbolism: the head formed of two serpent-heads facing each other, the bare breast upon which hangs a large necklace formed of hands and hearts, the skirt fastened with a belt which is also serpentine and supported in the middle by a skull, and the feet and hands terminating in animal claws. Under her feet, and

therefore invisible, is a carved reproduction of the monster of the earth. This is because the goddess represents the earth itself, old and always fertile, which first creates and later destroys all that which exists.

According to legend the mortal woman Coatlicue, a widow, lived at Tula and had one daughter and innumerable sons. One day on sweeping the temple she found a feather, which she placed under her belt; a short time later she realised that she was pregnant. When her daughter and sons noticed this, blind with fury over this maternal sin, they prepared to kill her. Coatlicue then heard the voice of her yet-unborn son telling her not to fear. She was immediately delivered of her son, fully grown and armed like the classic Athena, who in an instant had cut off the head of his sister and put his innumerable brothers to flight. The newly born was the god Huitzilopochtli—the sun—who on rising in the east makes his sister the moon and brothers the stars vanish from the skies.

The statue of Coatlicue has been interpreted in many ways, but it is undoubtedly one of the most amazing pieces of Aztec art. Here, as Paul Westheim has said, the terrible is transformed into the sublime.

AZTEC FEATHER MOSAIC
Plate 59

Among the handicrafts which we have reason to believe were brought to the level of fine art in the final period before the Spanish conquest is the highly perishable one of feather work. Essentially this consists of a mosaic in which the design is formed of feathers from various birds and in a great range of colours that are juxtaposed with infinite care to form the composition. Using this technique, headdresses, adornments for the back, ceremonial shields and no doubt many other objects which have long since disintegrated were produced. It is highly unlikely that such an article will ever be recovered by archaeologists in the field since the humidity would have destroyed the delicate materials; we therefore have very few examples left and almost all are in foreign museums. Most of these, like the ones at the Vienna Museum, were presented by Moctezuma to Cortes who then sent them to his king, Charles V. The latter had just been elected Emperor of Germany, and so the objects finally landed in Vienna. A few other examples also exist, deriving from old collections. The one reproduced here, which is in the National Museum of Anthropology in Mexico City, is one of the simplest we know. It represents the head of the rain god with two scrolls forming the eyes, a long nose, and the mouth framed by a rectangle and showing triangular teeth. This probably was a ceremonial shield. It is 19 cm. in diameter.

AZTEC STONE SCULPTURE
Plate 60

The Aztecs were the first people of Mesoamerica to produce sculpture to compare with that of the Olmecs some two thousand years before, though naturally it differed in style from that of their early forbears. While it is true that the majority of Aztec carvings depict gods or themes related to religion, we also find a number of pieces with an entirely different concept. Some small and admirably executed sculptures suggest that the artists were seeking aesthetically satisfying and not functional objects; we can almost speak of art for art's sake, which would indicate a remarkable urban evolution. Another group of carvings reveal a frankly political ideology and an imperialistic accent. For example, the enormous monolith around which are carved in low relief scenes portraying conquests of the Emperor Tizoc is undoubtedly a votive stone dedicated to the military triumphs of this emperor, and in its context recalls the well-known Column of Trajan in Rome.

On the stone illustrated here we have a combination of religious and political motifs. In the square constituting the lower part appears the date Eight Reed, with the name in the middle and the eight disks indicating the number. It refers to the year 1487 when the Emperor Ahuitzotl began his reign; we see him in the upper right-hand corner identified by the hieroglyph of a small animal of the same name, which is considered troublesome and dangerous to this day. Facing Ahuitzotl is his predecessor, the Emperor Tizoc, also with the identifying hieroglyph behind his head, in the form of a human foot. Both are performing the orthodox ritual on their person, which requires that blood be extracted from an ear by piercing it with a sharp instrument. Between the two figures appear the emblems of sacrifice—a ball of grass into which have been inserted two spines that have already been used; blood drips at the sides and below between two incense-burners, the long handles of which terminate in serpent-heads. Beneath is a strip decorated with drops and disks. The stone as a whole refers to the final dedication, in the reign of Ahuitzotl, of the Main Temple of Mexico City. Tizoc also appears in the scene because he initiated the construction, although he died before it was finished.

PYRAMID OF QUETZALCOATL, TEOTIHUACÁN
Plate 1 (Frontispiece)

Of the many buildings at Teotihuacán the most spectacular is that known as the Temple of Quetzalcoatl. Situated south-east of the Street of the Dead, it forms part of a vast complex which is partly religious and partly civil. The latter probably included the market—always centrally located in a Mesoamerican city—with its intense activity. There all the commercial transactions were carried out, since the concept of a shop as we understand it did not exist. The market was also a social centre: here news was exchanged, one met and chatted with friends, ate a meal perhaps and generally spent many a pleasant hour.

The centre of the sacred precincts was the great temple that crowned the pyramid, part of which we see in the plate. The temple no longer exists but on the base is still preserved a great part of its splendid sculpture. On each level—formed as usual with *talud* and *tablero* (see plate 9)—there stand out in high relief the heads of two gods: the plumed serpent, Quetzalcoatl, which is shown complete since its body meanders along the slopes and panels, and what is believed to represent the God of Rain, Tlaloc, but may be another deity, sometimes referred to as 'the god with a bow in the headdress'. These two heads are adorned with shells and other marine objects associated with water, that indispensable necessity for a society based on agriculture. The low balustrade of the large central staircase is also decorated with projecting heads.

This part, in which architecture is combined with sculpture, was built in Period II of Teotihuacán, perhaps around the time of Christ, when the city was nearing its zenith. Of the buildings on the Street of the Dead those that are constructed in the most severe style can be dated to Period III.

INDEX OF PLACES

Page numbers in italic type refer to the captions to the plates